o come, o come, emmanuel

AN ADVENT STUDY

LIFEWAY WOMEN

LifeWay Press®
Nashville, Tennessee

Published by LifeWay Press® • © 2020 LifeWay Christian Resources • Nashville, TN

ISBN: 978-1-0877-1571-1 • Item: 005826668
Dewey decimal classification: 242.33
Subject headings: ADVENT/JESUS CHRIST—NATIVITY/CHRISTMAS

Unless indicated otherwise, all Scripture taken from the Christian Standard Bible®, Copyright © 2017 by Holman Bible Publishers. Used by permission. Christian Standard Bible® and CSB® are federally registered trademarks of Holman Bible Publishers. Scripture taken from the New King James Version®. Copyright © 1982 by Thomas Nelson. Used by permission. All rights reserved. Scriptures marked KJV are taken from the KING JAMES VERSION (KJV): KING JAMES VERSION, public domain. Scriptures marked YLT are taken from Young's Literal Translation, public domain.

To order additional copies of this resource, write to LifeWay Church Resources Customer Service; One LifeWay Plaza; Nashville, TN 37234; order online at www.lifeway.com; fax 615.251.5933; phone toll free 800.458.2772; or email orderentry@lifeway.com.

Printed in the United States of America

Adult Ministry Publishing • LifeWay Church Resources • One LifeWay Plaza • Nashville, TN 37234

Cover design by Lauren Ervin

EDITORIAL TEAM, LIFEWAY WOMEN PUBLISHING

Becky Loyd
Director, LifeWay Women

Tina Boesch
Manager, LifeWay Women Bible Studies

Sarah Doss
Team Leader, LifeWay Women Bible Studies

Erin Davis
Content Editor

Emily Chadwell
Production Editor

Chelsea Waack
Graphic Designer

Contents

How to Use This Study

Welcome! We are eager to celebrate the season of Advent alongside you.

Since many Bible study groups don't meet during this busy season, we've created a study you can do alone, with family, or with your friends. Along with daily personal study, we provided activities each week you may choose to do by yourself or with others. Each week you'll find:

- an introduction;
- five days of personal study;
- activities to do individually, with kids and teens, or with your friends and family;
- group discussion questions.

This study is designed to help you shift your focus toward Emmanuel—God with us. Use the five days of personal study to reflect, allowing God's Word to nourish your soul.

GROUP DISCUSSION

If you decide to do this study with others, use the Group Guide discussion questions found at the end of each week to guide your conversation. In addition to answering the questions in the Group Guide, invite women to share the things they learned from each day of study and share how each week's Scriptures impacted them.

Invite women to share how they've incorporated the kids, teens, and adult activities into the season of Advent. If you choose, your group may want to bring the supplies needed and do one of the activities in a group setting as you discuss the Group Guide questions and personal study.

Because Advent can be a busy season, we hope the activities in the study provide a time of rest and reflection. Enjoy sharing the love of Jesus with your family, friends, and neighbors this season.

A GROUP TIME MIGHT LOOK SOMETHING LIKE THIS:

- Welcome (Use this time to light a candle if you choose to include an Advent wreath each week.)
- Ask the questions on the Group Guide page for that week.
- Review the five days of personal study.
- Ask women to share any special activities they added to their week as they focused on Advent.
- Read Scripture related to the week's theme. You can find a list of Scriptures for each week of Advent on page 142.
- Close in prayer.

SHARE WITH OTHERS

There may be those in your neighborhood or community who don't understand Advent. Consider inviting others to join you, using the Group Guide questions and hosting a group in your home. Explain the Advent wreath, what the Bible says about Jesus, and how your celebration of the Christmas season is different because of Christ.

Introduction

"Rejoice! Rejoice! Emmanuel shall come to thee, O Israel."[1]

This year, we've experienced sorrow on a global scale. Perhaps you're reading these words years after they were originally written, but you no doubt remember the coronavirus pandemic that swept our world into a season of fear, death, and heartache.

Every year, no matter the scale, we all experience sorrow—individually and communally. Every year holds its share of loneliness, hurt, and tragedy—of *brokenness*. This year, and every year, as the days on our calendar dwindle, our hearts cry out with some of the last words in the Bible, "Come, Lord Jesus!" (Rev. 22:20b).

Advent is a season set aside to celebrate that Christ came to us as a baby wrapped in swaddling clothes, and to look forward with anticipation to the moment when He will return as our triumphant King. It's a season to rejoice!

We've chosen the hymn "O Come, O Come, Emmanuel" as the theme for this Bible study. It's a song that has been sung by Christ's followers for more than 150 years. I love the verbs found in the chorus. (Hang with me.) *The call to rejoice is present tense.*

"REJOICE! REJOICE!"

This is a call to action. *Rejoice now, O Israel!* Sing praise! Be full of joy! Celebrate!

The second sentence of the chorus is future tense.

"EMMANUEL *SHALL* COME TO THEE, O ISRAEL" (EMPHASIS ADDED).

These familiar lyrics emphasize the past, the time before Christ's first coming. They help us remember that Israel, God's chosen people, once longed for Him to come and rescue them. God's children have been united by the same heart cry throughout the years, "Come, Lord Jesus!" Come be with us.

While they lived in loneliness, in sorrow, in hurt, in tragedy, in the sheer brokenness of our world, Israel begged God to send a savior. *But even as they pleaded for rescue, they rejoiced.*

Though it's a precious piece of church history, this song isn't Scripture. Though it wasn't God-breathed, it accurately reflects the stories of God's people recorded in the Old Testament, as well as the longings of our hearts today.

Israel could rejoice as they cried out for a savior because they believed in the promises of God. Our God is faithful, and we know He will fulfill every word He has spoken. Jesus Christ fulfilled all the promises of God (2 Cor. 1:20). So His people can rejoice in what's to come.

In the same way, even in seasons of uncertainty when the brokenness of our world weighs heavily upon us, we can rejoice too. We can be a people full of joy even now. Emmanuel will come to us again. We can trust it because He said it. He promised, "Yes, I am coming soon" (Rev. 22:20a).

As we look back at the stable where Jesus arrived that first Christmas, we can rejoice, celebrating another promise kept. As we look forward, longing for the day of Christ's second coming, we can celebrate with singing. Though we mourn in lonely exile here, we celebrate with great hope that the Son of God will soon appear.

Now, and always, "Rejoice! Rejoice! Emmanuel shall come to thee, O Israel."

emmanuel

WEEK 1

O COME, O COME, EMMANUEL

by Elizabeth Hyndman

Before we go any further, the grammarian in me wants to address the spelling issue we have in this study. In the title, we've spelled Emmanuel like the hymn. But you'll see Christ often referenced as "Immanuel" as well. Why the discrepancy?"

The explanation is simple—in Hebrew, the original word looks more like "Immanuel," while in Greek, the transliteration of the word is typically spelled "Emmanuel." The New Testament, largely written in Greek originally, therefore sometimes translates the name with an E, while the Old Testament, originally written in Hebrew, translates it with an I.

The name Emmanuel carries great significance in the life of God's people. Emmanuel means "God is with us" (Matt. 1:23). No matter how you spell it, Emmanuel is a promise.

In the holiday season, we remember the value of time together—physical presence. Joy shared.

Throughout Scripture, God displays a desire to be with His people. He fellowshipped with Adam and Eve in the garden. He went with the nation of

Israel as they fled Egypt, leading them through the wilderness with fire and cloud. He tabernacled with His people in the desert. He dwelt among them in the temple in Jerusalem.

Throughout history, God's people have also had glimpses of life when they felt without His presence—the temple was destroyed; the people were in exile; the prophets fell silent.

A verse of the beloved carol speaks to these moments: "And ransom captive Israel, that mourns in lonely exile here, until the Son of God appear."[2] They waited in mourning, in captivity—literally and figuratively. Yet they did not wait without hope. They held on to the promise of Emmanuel. Surely they whispered, "God will be with us again." And He is! Jesus Christ, God with us, came in physical form to dwell among us.

Today we rest in a new promise—the promise of a second coming. Because He lives within us, we never have to know life without God's presence. Even so, our hearts long for Emmanuel. We look forward with great anticipation to the day when we will once again experience His physical presence—God with us, *forever.*

Consider the specific ways the word *Emmanuel* has been a part of your Christmas traditions. Include favorite carols, decorations, and holiday festivities.

Do you sense God's presence more or less during the Christmas season, compared with the rest of the year? Explain.

How does God's desire to be with His people comfort you in this season?

Consider Psalm 16:11. According to this verse, where is joy truly found in this—and every—season?

If you want the Advent season to be one of enjoying the Lord's presence, tell Him so. Close your time with prayer, asking God to give you a greater awareness of His presence and thanking Him that He is Emmanuel, God with us.

GOD WITH US IN THE GARDEN

by Faith C. Whatley

First, read Genesis 3:1-7.

I'll never forget April 20, 1999. My memory takes me back there in the blink of an eye. I can recall the moment I landed on the island of Oahu, Hawaii, like it was yesterday. It was my first visit to Hawaii, and I was overtaken by the island's beauty. It truly is paradise. My host for the weekend picked me up from the airport and drove me to the apartment where I would be staying. There I was, on the sixteenth floor in a corner apartment with floor-to-ceiling windows, overlooking Waikiki Beach. I was mesmerized by the beautiful view. My mind could hardly take it in.

As I started to unpack, I turned on the TV to catch up on the news. I heard something that I could not believe—there had been a shooting at Columbine High School and students had been killed. What we didn't know in 1999 was that many more school shootings would happen in the years to come. On that day, it was the most horrific thing I had ever heard. I was thirty-five years old at the time and had two small children. I sat down in disbelief and thought, *How can I be in this beautiful, majestic place when something so terrible has happened?* It felt like a bad dream. I wanted to wake up and realize the tragedy didn't really happen. But it did happen.

When I read Genesis 1–3, I wonder if Adam and Eve felt the same way. Did they want to believe they were in a bad dream and wake up to discover they hadn't really chosen to listen to the evil one and disobey the God who made them? Those times when I've missed the mark God has set for me, I've felt my stomach drop. I imagine Adam and Eve must have wanted to close their eyes and forget the fact that their sin had fractured their perfect relationship with God. But they couldn't—because of their rebellion against God's command, sin entered paradise. I wonder if they thought, *How could we have been given such a beautiful place to live in and experience something so terrible?* It must have felt surreal.

Have you ever experienced a moment like this, when the consequences of your sin felt like a bad dream? Write about it below.

The garden of Eden may feel like a strange place to begin this Advent season. We want the warm fuzzies of the season, not the angst of the fall of man. Yet when we read the first chapters of Genesis we see that God created a beautiful place for humanity to flourish. This is a love story, not just between man and woman, but between the God of the universe and His creation. As we enter this season of giving, consider God's elaborate gifts:

- He created the heavens and the earth and everything that would live there.
- He created humankind in His image.
- He placed Adam in a beautiful, perfect garden, free of all sin and shame.
- He created Eve so Adam would not be alone.
- He created marriage, the first family.
- Everything He created was a good and perfect gift (Jas. 1:17).

And perhaps the most elaborate gift of all—from the dawn of humanity, God has given us His presence. He did not separate Himself from all that He made. He walked and talked with Adam on the footpaths of Eden.

We all know what happened next. Because of Adam and Eve's disobedience, God administered painful consequences. The first image bearers were banished from the perfect home God had created for them. I wonder if they looked around after in disbelief, shell-shocked by what happened.

Their rebellion was real. So were the consequences. We still feel the impact today. Yet even in their sin, God never abandoned them. Not for a second. They went on to create a family "with the Lord's help" (Gen. 4:1). God never turned His back on Adam and Eve. He never stopped loving them. The rest of the Bible reveals that God did not withdraw the gift of His presence from humankind. From the garden to the Gospels and beyond, we find God walking and talking with the children He made in His image.

What other evidence do you find in Scripture that God did not withdraw His presence from humankind because of the fall?

Have you ever paused to consider what a mercy it is that God still invites us into His presence, even though we are sinners (Heb. 10:19-22)?

Yes, intimacy with God changed when sin entered the picture, but we still serve a God who offers His presence. The love story continued when Christ went to the cross to pay the penalty for sin, making a way for us to come back to the perfect relationship God intended all along.

End today's devotional by writing out a prayer expressing your desire to experience more of God's presence in this Advent season.

GOD WITH US IN THE CLOUD

by Jessica Yentzer

First, read Exodus 13:21-22.

Life will always throw us curveballs. When I find myself in circumstances that I don't know how to navigate, I am incredibly grateful for the story of the Israelites we get to examine together today. Their story reminds us that in times of uncertainty, difficulty, and pain, we can find hope by fixing our eyes on the God who chooses to be present with us. When we examine Scripture and see examples of God showing up over and over again for His people, we're reminded He will do the same for us.

> Are there circumstances you are currently walking through that make you long for reminders of the hope found in Christ? List them below.

> How does the fact that God continually showed up for His people throughout Scripture encourage you today?

Let's consider the context of Exodus 13:21-22. The Israelites had just watched God unleash the plagues in Egypt, and Pharaoh had finally agreed to let them go, ending a four-hundred-year period of slavery for God's people. Exodus 13:17-18 reveals that God led the Israelites on a specific path away from Egypt.

READ EXODUS 13:17-18.

Why did God lead the Israelites on an unconventional path out of Egypt (v. 17)?

In Exodus 13:21 we learn one of the purposes of God's presence in the cloud—to guide the people. The pillar of cloud became a pillar of fire at night "so that they could travel day or night." In verse 22 we learn that the pillar didn't leave its place in front of the people. In other words, the presence of God was with His children every step of the way.

How do you see God's presence currently guiding your steps?

How have you seen God's presence change the path you would have normally taken?

Just a few verses later, we read that Pharaoh and his army decided to pursue the Israelites.

READ EXODUS 14:10-11.

How did the Israelites react when they saw the Egyptians approaching?

For those of us who know how this story ends, it's easy to be dismissive of the Israelites' fear. We may read this account with a strong desire to remind the Israelites that they were being led by the God who had just brought the plagues on Egypt and delivered them from hundreds of years of slavery! But how many times have our circumstances felt so overwhelming that fear overtakes our trust in the God who faithfully leads us?

As the story unfolds, the Lord commanded Moses to part the Red Sea so the Israelites could walk through on dry ground, escaping Pharaoh's army. Before they took even a single step on the sandy floor, the pillar of cloud moved behind the Israelites, creating an impenetrable barrier between them and the Egyptians.

> It came between the Egyptian and Israelite forces. There was cloud and darkness, it lit up the night, and neither group came near the other all night long.

EXODUS 14:20

What an amazing display of God's power! While the Israelites probably would have preferred He not even allow the Egyptians to come after them, God was able to demonstrate His power to the Egyptians *and* the Israelites by parting the Red Sea and rescuing His people.

Once the Israelites arrived safely on the other side, the Lord closed the sea over the Egyptians, destroying them. The Israelites' response revealed that their gaze had shifted away from their circumstances and toward the Lord:

> When Israel saw the great power that the LORD used against the Egyptians, the people feared the LORD and believed in him and in his servant Moses.

EXODUS 14:31

Recall a time when seeing the Lord's power at work shifted your perspective. Write about it below. How can you more consistently remember His sovereignty and be encouraged by it?

I am thankful to serve a God who constantly reminds me that He is greater than what I fear. It's an everyday battle for me to fix my eyes on the Lord rather than the difficulties around me. But when I read the story of the Israelites, I clearly see the Lord's faithful presence and am encouraged. As an observer looking in from the outside, it's so clear to me how essential the Lord's presence was to their journey. He came near to them in the cloud, and He is near to us today.

My hope is that you begin to crave and rely on the Lord's presence in the days ahead. Be encouraged by the truth that He desires to be near to you.

> **Where did you see God's presence in your life this week? How can you shift your vision to see Him more often in your day-to-day living?**

GOD WITH US IN THE TABERNACLE AND TEMPLE

by Rachel Forrest

𝔉irst, read 𝔈xodus 40:34-38.

Have you ever seen a thunderhead? A thunderhead is a large, column-like cloud with big rounded puffs. (They resemble a head of cauliflower). They usually build and appear before an advancing thunderstorm. Living in Oklahoma, in the heart of "Tornado Alley," I've seen some massive thunderheads. They always amaze me, as their density and height reveal the vast expanse of the sky. They also strike me with foreboding apprehension as I anticipate the coming storm. The greater the thunderhead, the more powerful the storm.

When I was a young girl, I used to stare at thunderheads in wonder. They often catch the light of the sun just right and look like they're on fire. Sometimes they pass in front of the sun and their edges become ablaze with a "silver lining." When this happened, my childish understanding believed the clouds were concealing heaven, and if I could just peak behind them, I could see that glorious city. A blazing thunderhead is the mental image I picture when I read about the presence of God in the tabernacle in Exodus.

After He delivered the people of Israel from Egypt, God established a covenant with them through which they were uniquely chosen by Him to live for His purposes and His glory. He gave them a distinct set of laws so other nations would see that they were a peculiar people who lived differently than everyone around them. He also prescribed how and where they would worship, giving meticulous instructions for the construction of a house of worship, a tabernacle (also called the tent of meeting). Exodus 35 records some of the instructions for building the tabernacle and the specific items that would be housed within it.

Look closely at the following verses in Exodus 35 (CSB) and fill in the blanks:

- Verse 5: "Take up an offering among you for the Lord. Let everyone _____ bring this as the Lord's offering."

- Verse 10: "Let all the _____ among you come and make everything that the Lord has commanded."

- Verse 22: "Both men and women came; _____ brought ... all kinds of gold jewelry—everyone who presented a presentation offering of gold to the Lord."

- Verse 26: "And all the _____ spun the goat hair by virtue of their skill."

- Verse 29: "So the Israelites brought a freewill offering to the Lord, _____ to bring something for all the work that the Lord, through Moses, had commanded to be done."

Moses told the people that those "whose heart is willing" should provide the offerings for the work, and those who are "skilled artisans" or "skillful craftsmen" should make the items for the tabernacle. In other words, although they were all a part of God's chosen people, not just any Israelite could step up to do the work, only the men and women with the right gifts and the right attitude. Because this wasn't just any other tent or building.

READ EXODUS 29:42-46.

What was the purpose of the tabernacle?

The tabernacle would be the physical location of God's presence with His people. In this place, God would dwell among humankind and make Himself known. When Moses told the people that only those with the right heart attitude and skill set should contribute to the work on the tabernacle, he reflected the "otherness" of this place. They were building a holy structure, consecrated by God Himself (29:44). The word *consecrated* literally means "set apart."[3] Their rescuer and redeemer, the God who performed signs and wonders in delivering them from the oppression of the Egyptians, was setting apart a distinct place so that He could dwell among them (v. 46). God clearly wanted to be with His people, and He was making a way. What does it look like for a holy God to be present with His people? Take a look at Exodus 40.

READ EXODUS 40:34-38.

Underline every instance of "cloud" and "glory of the LORD."

Once construction of the tabernacle was complete, the people witnessed a cloud descending on it, and the glory of the Lord filled it. Throughout the Old Testament, this language is used to communicate God's presence. Earlier in Exodus, God appeared in a cloud and the glory of the Lord settled on Mount Sinai when He created His covenant with His people (Ex. 19). Later, at Solomon's dedication of the temple to the Lord, a cloud filled the temple and prevented the priests from entering because of the presence of the glory of the Lord (1 Kings 8:10-11; 2 Chron. 7:1-2). And in Ezekiel's vision of the temple, he described it as covered in a cloud and filled with the brightness of God's glory (Ezek. 10:4; 43:4-5). In each instance, God was present with His people.

When the people of God saw the cloud cover the tabernacle and temple, they knew God was with them. As they continued their journey toward the promised land, they had His presence to lead the way. Whenever they didn't see the cloud covering the tabernacle, they packed up their things and continued toward their new home. If the cloud remained over the tabernacle, they waited on the Lord to reveal the next steps (Ex. 40:36-37). The tabernacle was their compass, and the cloud of God's presence was their guide.

Yet even though God dwelt with His people, they could not approach Him freely. Here is one of the beautiful paradoxes of Scripture: while the cloud communicated God's presence, it also represented God's holiness. It was a protective barrier between a holy God and sinful man.

Look up the following verses. What do they reveal about the relationship between God and humanity?

- Exodus 26:33; 33:18-20

- Leviticus 16:2

- 1 Kings 8:11

The glory of God is so pure that humanity cannot even look at Him directly. In spite of this, God made a way for His people to experience His presence through the various chambers of the tabernacle and temple. Within the most holy place, the ark of the covenant—which stored the stone tablets (the physical elements of God's covenant with His people)—was contained behind a veil.

God desires to dwell with His people, and the tabernacle was a part of His plan for being present among them. Nevertheless, His holiness prevented His people from being able to approach Him freely and whenever they chose. His holiness remains unchanged today. Our sin still separates us from a holy God. However, just like in the tabernacle and the temple, God made a way for us to enter His presence.

READ HEBREWS 4:14-16; 10:19-23.

Write a prayer of thanksgiving to God for giving us His Son, Jesus, who removes all barriers and gives us confident access to the throne of grace.

Day 4

GOD WITH US

by Erin Franklin

First, read Luke 1:26-38.

I wouldn't necessarily say I grew up in a "musical" family, but that didn't stop us from always having music in our home, even if that simply meant someone was whistling, piano-playing, humming, or singing as he or she went about the day. We were no von Trapps, but we still sang. My little brother, in particular, would constantly sing to himself. Looking back, I fondly see this as just his way of expressing the little-boy joy in his heart.

But during my teenage years, it annoyed me to hear him singing to himself while we worked on homework at the kitchen table. I wanted peace and quiet! My mother recalls that one day I exclaimed in a fit of exasperation at his incessant song, "Andrew, you think you live in a musical!"

It's a funny moment to think back on now, but it's also easy for me to see how simple it is to lose reflexive childlike joy as I get older. Joy doesn't often feel automatic, but thankfully we have a Savior who understands. In the spirit of Advent, let's take a look at an unconventional family and see how they, despite earthly trials and worries, celebrated Emmanuel's coming with joy.

In Luke 1, we read that the angel Gabriel came to visit Mary and announced, "The Lord is with you" (v. 28). Biblical commentator Robert Stein writes, "This is not a wish ('may the Lord be with you') but a statement and refers to God's mighty power being present and upon Mary."[4] Initially, the gravity of these words—this imperative statement—troubled Mary, but the angel reassured her not to be afraid because she had "found favor with God" (v. 30).

When Mary heard what she had been called to do, she faithfully submitted, trusting that even though this was quite possibly one of the most traumatic things a young, betrothed Jewish girl could experience, God had a plan.

READ LUKE 1:39-56.

Why do you think Mary lifted up a song of praise?

Sometimes troubles crowd out our joy, and our joy needs a little nudge. It wasn't until after Elizabeth's affirmation to Mary that Mary's joy overflowed, and she sang her song of praise. Maybe people around Mary didn't understand why she was acting like she was living in a musical, randomly bursting into song. But when we truly allow ourselves to experience the presence of Emmanuel, God with us, we cannot help but be filled with joy, even when trials beset us. Even baby John the Baptist, in innocent and automatic infantile joy, leapt in Elizabeth's womb when he first experienced the presence of Jesus (vv. 41,44). Elizabeth's words of encouragement can also serve as a reminder to lift up our sisters in Christ, to help relinquish their burdens so they can fully experience the presence of God.

What is a daily action of praise you can take this season to make sure you don't lose sight of the call to joy? Is it like Mary's song of praise? Like Elizabeth's blessing and words of affirmation? Something else?

Next, let's take a look at how Joseph responded to the news of Mary's pregnancy.

READ MATTHEW 1:18-25.

What had Joseph resolved to do before the angel spoke to him?

What did he do after the angel spoke to him?

The passage we just read doesn't explicitly say this, but I think we can imagine from Joseph's inward resolve to divorce Mary quietly that he wasn't filled with an abundance of joy at the thought of his fiancée's pregnancy.

Again, here we see someone facing what seems to be an insurmountable trial. Sometimes it's hard for us, like Joseph, to have joy during difficult trials. It may even seem impossible. But that's when we, hard as it may be, have the opportunity to trust that God's ways are greater than ours.

We need faith that joy will come in the morning (Ps. 30:5). Joseph may not have had joy in his heart initially, but he trusted God's plan was better than his. The angel told Joseph to name the child Emmanuel, which means "God with us" (Matt. 1:23). Joseph likely couldn't comprehend the miraculousness of this name's significance at the time, but he trusted he would one day. There is great joy in simple faithfulness.

Have you ever been through a difficult trial in which joy seemed absent, and you had to trust that God's ways were bigger than yours—holding fast to the faith that joy would come in the morning? Describe it below.

Next, let's look at the baby of this unconventional family.

READ JOHN 1:1,14.

Young's Literal Translation puts John 1:14 this way:

> And the Word became flesh, and did tabernacle among us, and we beheld his glory, glory as of an only begotten of a father, full of grace and truth.

I find it interesting that some of the most literal translations include the word "tabernacle." The original Greek word is *skēnoō*, which means "(specially), to reside (as God did in the Tabernacle of old, a symbol of protection and communion):—dwell."[5]

For the original readers already familiar with the Old Testament, the use of this word would remind them of how God came and dwelt with the Israelites in the tabernacle. The word choice is special because it symbolizes Jesus' holy dwelling with us. Just like the tabernacle occupied the center of the community in the Old Testament, Jesus came to dwell with us on earth, right in the center of everything.

What does God dwelling with us have to do with joy?

Christ tabernacling among us is the beautiful picture of God's closeness when the Word became flesh. Because of this closeness, Jesus shares in our weaknesses. He sympathizes with our struggles. He rejoices with us. He understands from living with us that our fleshly dwelling on earth is not always easy, but with faith for the joy ahead, we can endure and lift up our praise to the Father.

> For the joy that lay before him, he endured the cross, despising the shame, and sat down at the right hand of the throne of God.

HEBREWS 12:2b

When we feel troubled and fearful like Mary initially was, or disappointed and disheartened like Joseph may have been, remember: God is with us; we don't have to be afraid. We can seek to live a Christian life similar to that of a child who can't help but reflexively sing or leap for the joy in his heart. We can shout for joy and gladness because Jesus came to dwell among us!

GOD WITH US IN THE INDWELLING OF THE HOLY SPIRIT

by Karen Jones

𝔉irst, read John 14:12-17.

I left U.S. soil for the first time on a church mission trip to Namur, Belgium. I was fully equipped with a sleep mask, earplugs, and Benadryl for our overnight flight, but try as I might, I could not sleep. When we arrived, John, one of the missionaries we were working with, determined to keep us awake to get us over jet lag quickly. I've never wanted to sleep more in my life, but John hiked us across Namur and up to the Citadel overlooking the city.

John told us about the spiritual darkness in Western Europe while we sat on benches, admiring the river and the beautiful European buildings covering the landscape. I was about to nod off right there on that bench with the wind whipping around me when John said something that woke me up in more ways than one. He told us that our presence in Namur was bringing light into that dark place—just us merely being there. Even if we didn't hand out a single Bible, say a single prayer, or speak to a single person, our presence in that city would still bring light.

John 14 is part of Jesus' farewell discourse. We learn from Matthew 1:23 that Jesus is Emmanuel, God with us. John 1:14 tells us that Jesus is the Word made flesh who dwelt among us, but in John 14, Jesus knew He would soon be returning to the Father. The cross was near, and He would soon do the work of salvation God had sent Him to earth to accomplish. But before He left, Jesus had some important things He wanted to say to His followers.

> **Look back at verse 12. What did Jesus say about the works of those who believe in Him?**

Jesus said we would do even greater works than He did! If it weren't right there in the Bible I wouldn't believe it, but God's Word is true.

How can our works be greater than that of Jesus? Look at verses 16 and 17. Who did Jesus say He would ask the Father to give us?

The Counselor. The Helper. The Advocate. Different versions translate this word in verse 16 differently, but almost all of them use "the Spirit of truth" in verse 17. Jesus was promising us the Holy Spirit. Our works can be greater than those of Jesus because of the Holy Spirit in us. Isn't that amazing to think about?

John used the Greek word *menō* in both verse 16 and verse 17. The CSB translates it "be with" in verse 16 and "remains" in verse 17. *Menō* means to abide, not to depart, not to leave, to continue to be present.[6] The Holy Spirit abides in us. He is staying with us. He is in us. He isn't going anywhere.

Look again at verse 16. How long can we expect the Holy Spirit to be with us?

Now, jump down a few verses and take a look at John 14:25-26.

Jesus went back to the Father, but He didn't leave His followers alone. Jesus asked the Father, and the Father sent the Holy Spirit in the name of the Son. All three persons of the Trinity worked together to ensure we are never alone and without God.

Notice the work the Holy Spirit does in us. He teaches us all things and reminds us of Jesus' words. Jesus spoke again in John about the work of the Holy Spirit.

READ JOHN 16:7-11.

Write down the three things Jesus said the Counselor, the Helper, the Advocate would convict the world of.

Not only is the Holy Spirit at work in us, teaching us and reminding us of God's truth, but He is also at work in the broken world around us, convicting people of sin, righteousness, and judgment.

Look at 2 Corinthians 1:22. What does this verse say about God's gift of the Holy Spirit?

Take a look at Ephesians 1:13-14. What do these verses tell us about the Holy Spirit?

We, as believers, are not only indwelt by the Holy Spirit but are sealed in Him. The Holy Spirit is our guarantee, or down payment, of our inheritance. What is this inheritance? Verse 14 tells us briefly that it is "the redemption of the possession." What does that mean exactly?

READ ROMANS 8:12-17.

What is the Spirit we have received?

We have received the Spirit of adoption. God has made us part of His family. We are God's children! As God's children, we are coheirs with Christ! We will share in Christ's suffering as we walk through this broken world, but we look forward to the day we will be glorified with Him.

READ ROMANS 8:18-23.

What does verse 23 say we are waiting for?

Is this a little confusing? We read in verse 15 that we have received the Spirit of adoption, but here in verse 23 we are waiting for our adoption? My friends, we live in the already/not yet. Jesus has done the work of redemption. We have been sealed with the Holy Spirit, the guarantee of our redemption, but we are awaiting that final redemption when Jesus will return and right every wrong and make everything that was broken new again. Then we will be united with Him forever.

READ REVELATION 21:3.

Do any of the words in this verse remind you of what you learned on Day 3 about the tabernacle?

God will tabernacle among us. He will dwell with us forever. This is what we are longing for, what the Holy Spirit guarantees, when our adoption will be finalized, when we receive our long-awaited inheritance, when we are glorified, when we are finally with God the Father, God the Son, and God the Holy Spirit forever.

God was with His people in the garden. God was with His people in the cloud. God was with His people in the tabernacle and temple. God is with His people in the Son through the Holy Spirit. And while we walk by the Spirit, we await the coming day when we will be with God in our heavenly home for all eternity.

So let's go back to my friend John's assertion that our mere presence in spiritually dark Western Europe brought light. Was he correct? Absolutely! Dear friend, you have the very Spirit of the living God dwelling in you, abiding in you. Everywhere you go, the Spirit goes with you, not only reminding you of truth and empowering you to walk in it, but convicting the world around you of its need for the Savior.

How have you seen God coming close to you? In you? Around you? Ask the Holy Spirit to wake you up and give you eyes to see.

NOTES

O COME, O COME, EMMANUEL

MAKE HOMEMADE

Cinnamon Salt Dough Ornaments

by Larissa Arnault Roach

Is there a time of year when we feel God more with us than Christmas? When we get into the holiday spirit and feel cozy while cuddled under a quilt sipping a hot beverage, that safe, warm feeling reminds us that God is near. What's more, His presence in us means we now have the pleasing aroma of Christ. Second Corinthians 2:15 says, "For to God we are the fragrance of Christ among those who are being saved and among those who are perishing." As you make these ornaments and the scents of the season fill your home, think on 2 Corinthians 2:15 and thank God for the gift of His Son.

GATHER

- 2 cups plain flour
- 1 cup salt
- ½ cup cinnamon
- 1 to 1½ cups warm water
- Rolling pin
- Cookie cutters
- Skewer or small coffee straw
- String or twine

DIRECTIONS

1. Set your oven to the lowest possible temperature (170 degrees).

2. Combine the flour, salt, and cinnamon. Form a well in the center.

3. Slowly add the water and mix until a dough forms. Start with one cup, adding more as needed. If the dough seems a bit runny, allow the mixture to rest for a few moments before adding more flour. The salt will absorb some extra moisture. However, you don't want it to be gooey and sticky, so start with less water and add as needed. The dough should be close to the consistency of Play-Doh.

4. Roll out the dough ¼-inch thick. Using cookie cutters (smaller sizes work well), cut out ornament shapes.

5. Use a skewer or small straw to create a hole for the string to add later. Consider whether you are using these ornaments as gift tags, a garland, or tree ornaments when placing the holes.

6. Arrange the ornaments on a baking sheet and bake in the oven for one hour. Flip and bake another hour.

7. Allow to cool. Using pretty string, create a garland, tie on packages, or hang on the tree.

NOTES:

- Although cinnamon salt dough is safe to taste, it is not edible.

- Mix up the scents! Add spices like ginger, clove, and nutmeg if you like. Or add a few drops (about 10) of an essential oil like orange or pine.

- If you would prefer, you can air dry the ornaments for twenty-four hours rather than baking.

- These ornaments can also be painted!

- Due to the preservative nature of salt, these homemade ornaments can last a long time. When you are ready to pack up your Christmas decor, carefully wrap them up in tissue paper and place them in an airtight container.

REMEMBERING

God's Presence

by Michelle Prater Freeman

On social media, the holidays seem full of lights and laughter. But behind the scenes, these days are often full of loneliness too. Thankfully, the Advent season offers us the name Emmanuel again and again, a gentle reminder that we are never alone.

Have you ever been in a room full of people but felt incredibly alone at the same time? In our ever-connected society, we might expect loneliness to be dying, but instead it is alive and well. Your teen has likely felt its weight on days when he missed the invite to the best Christmas party or the acceptance letter to a top college where his friends are headed. When he is feeling left out and misunderstood, or when he is tempted to fill the loneliness with the wrong people, he may need to be reminded of the power of Jesus' name: Emmanuel, God with us.

Sit down with your teen this week and talk about the reality of loneliness. Then revisit all the incredible steps God has taken to be present with His people. Instead of placing us alone on an island, "The Word became flesh and dwelt among us" (John 1:14a). With your teen, brainstorm a list of ways God has shown up throughout his life. Maybe prayer calmed his preschool heart when nightmares occurred. Or maybe God used His church to support your family during a hard time. Help your teen recognize evidence of God's presence and provision during each life stage, including the sometimes lonely days of adolescence.

One gift of Advent is the repeated reminder of Christ's birth. Let that reminder combat any loneliness this season brings. God sent His Son on that glorious day long ago, knowing He would be a Comforter during your teen's childhood years and an Encourager as the realities of adulthood loom large ahead. We are not alone. Through it all, Emmanuel is with us.

JESUS

Is Near

by Shelly D. Harris

Since creation, God has pursued a relationship with people. We were created to know and love God, yet sin broke our relationship with Him. So God sent His one and only Son to dwell with us—to be our Emmanuel.

DIRECTIONS

Play the following game using the baby Jesus figurine from a child-friendly nativity set. Hide the baby Jesus figurine somewhere in your house. Challenge family members to take turns searching for it. Call out clues of "near" or "far" as everyone searches. Celebrate when the figurine is found. Allow another family member to help you hide the figurine and play again.

Gather to debrief the game: The good news is that we never have to search for God like we did in our game. God is with us. Read Matthew 1:18-23. Explain to your family that Emmanuel is a special name for Jesus that means "God with us." This special name reminds us that Jesus came to earth to rescue people from their sin. One day Jesus will return, and we will be with Him forever. Until then, the Holy Spirit lives inside everyone who has repented of their sin and trusted Jesus as their Lord and Savior.

Invite everyone to name a time they need to remember that God is with us (e.g., when they are afraid of the dark, when they tell someone about Jesus).

Close by praying: *Thank You, God, for sending Jesus to dwell on earth and pay the price for our sin. Thank You for the gift of the Holy Spirit, who lives inside all who know and love Jesus as their Lord and Savior. You are always near to us, and we know we can trust You. Amen.*

dayspring

O COME, THOU DAYSPRING

by Elizabeth Hyndman

In the northern hemisphere, it's easy to grasp the concept of darkness during Advent season. The darkest day of the year is only a few days before Christmas. The literal darkness that surrounds us is a reminder of the spiritual darkness of our world.

The second verse of "O Come, O Come, Emmanuel" begins with a name for Jesus we don't use often—Dayspring. I love this old-fashioned word. It essentially means the beginning of the morning—when the day is "springing" up. It can also mean the beginning of a new era.

Ever since Genesis 3, our world has been filled with death ... with sin ... with destruction. In ancient times, God's people experienced wars, suffering, famine, natural disasters, pandemics, violence, hatred, and death. Since Adam and Eve disobeyed, the shadow of death has lurked around every corner. Because of sin, darkness has crept over the world. And since the garden of Eden, God's people have anticipated the morning.

The hymn's verse continues, "Come and cheer our spirits by Thine advent here; disperse the gloomy clouds of night, and death's dark shadows put to flight."[7]

In Luke 1, after John the Baptist was born, his father, Zechariah, sang a song of prophecy. In it, he said, "Because of our God's merciful compassion, the dawn from on high will visit us to shine on those who live in darkness and the shadow of death, to guide our feet into the way of peace" (vv. 78-79). Zechariah must have felt it in the deepest corners of his heart. After centuries of spiritual darkness, morning was coming.

The morning did come. Our Dayspring, Jesus Christ, ushered in a new era—an era where death was defeated and the darkness was overcome by the Light (John 1:5).

Today, after Jesus' death and resurrection and ascension, we still live in a broken world plagued by spiritual darkness. Even though we who believe have eternal life, we still experience the shadow of death all around us. And we know, deep down, this is not the way the world should be. In this night, we anticipate the morning.

We look forward, with hope, to the dawn of a new era—a world without death, destruction, and disease. We look forward to the Dayspring's return.

Reflect on the role light plays in your Christmas traditions.

Does the spiritual darkness of the world feel darker or brighter during Advent season? Explain.

Read Psalm 27:1 together. How does this verse point to the Christmas story recorded in the Gospels?

In order to celebrate the good news, we must wrestle with the reality of our sin nature. Are you more or less aware of your sin in this season? How can we encourage each other to live as children of the light?

Isaiah prophesied about the birth of Christ when he wrote, "The people walking in darkness have seen a great light; a light has dawned on those living in the land of darkness" (Isa. 9:2). Take time to thank the Lord together for rescuing you from the darkness of sin and being your light. Then close your time together by praying for those who continue to walk in spiritual darkness. Ask the Lord to woo them to Himself during this season.

THE DARKNESS OF THIS WORLD

by Morgan Hawk

First, read Romans 8:19-25.

We live in a dark world. And I don't just mean spiritually. I mean outside my window, it is literally dark at 3:30 in the afternoon. Somehow the limited light of the winter months can make us feel the spiritual darkness of our world more acutely. We are surrounded by so much darkness that it can be difficult to see the light. Parents get cancer, best friends struggle with infertility, children suffer, nations rage, and we just don't know what to do. The Book of Romans reveals that we are not the first Christ followers to grieve the state of the world.

Consider Romans 8:20. What has creation been subjected to?

If you're like me, you have a vague idea of what the word "futility" means. A quick dictionary lookup says *futile* means to be "completely ineffective."[8] What does that have to do with anything? Well, actually, everything.

Think back to Week 1. Together we considered the fact that the fall of man in Genesis 3 had some big, capital "C" consequences. Here's a quick refresher.

> And he said to the man, "Because you listened to your wife and ate
> from the tree about which I commanded you, 'Do not eat from it':
> The ground is cursed because of you. You will eat from it by means
> of painful labor all the days of your life."

GENESIS 3:17

When Adam disobeyed God, he ushered in consequences for all of humankind, and the ground was cursed right along with him. The earth is groaning and waiting with anticipation for God's full redemption. This is why the earth is futile, rendered ineffective, and eagerly awaiting change. All of creation, including us, is groaning in labor pains, waiting for the birth of new life, free from sin and its consequences. All mommas know labor pains are no joke. These are big hurts that we are facing, but they are pointing forward to the day of our deliverance.

This is not how it is supposed to be. This is not how the earth was created. Romans 8:20 reminds us that sin has subjected the earth to futility, but we are not without hope. With the pain of labor comes the birth of something new, and so is the hope for our world and for us.

We have hope that with the redemption of our bodies we will fulfill the final stage of adoption and be reunited with God. We have hope that a day is coming when God will make all things new, even this broken, groaning world. How can we hold on to hope on dark days when hope feels fleeting? Let's head back to Romans and read Paul's reminder:

> For we know that the whole creation has been groaning together with labor pains until now. Not only that, but we ourselves who have the Spirit as the firstfruits—we also groan within ourselves, eagerly waiting for adoption, the redemption of our bodies.

ROMANS 8:22-23

In speaking of the "firstfruits," Paul was assuring us of the promise of what is to come. We have received the Spirit as a down payment of the full redemption we will one day receive. Where there are first fruits, there are always seconds. God, who has already given us so much, has even more in store for His children. With the comfort from the Spirit, we can be assured of our hope in the Father even in the midst of our darkest days.

Look up the following verses. What does each verse reveal about the Spirit?

- 2 Corinthians 1:22; 5:5

- Ephesians 1:13-14

How does knowing the Spirit has been sent to God's people comfort you in times of darkness?

In the following passage, circle or highlight the word "hope" each time it is written.

Now in this hope we were saved, but hope that is seen is not hope, because who hopes for what he sees? Now if we hope for what we do not see, we eagerly wait for it with patience.

ROMANS 8:24-25

We are all looking for hope. We post the word to our social media feed and hang it on our walls. We hope there is still ice cream in the fridge when we get home. We hope traffic won't make us late for our appointment. But the hope Paul was describing is completely different. He was reminding us of the hope we have in Christ.

This hope is far greater than any other because it is not based on empty wishes. Our hope in Christ is based on His promises to restore. It is not a hope we can see, at least not yet. Our true hope is in the coming restoration of our world. The end of groaning and the redemption of God and His people. It's a hope that requires faith that God will keep His promises.

Before God created the world, all was darkness, and there was nothing except God. But God! He took darkness and created light.

We all face moments of spiritual and emotional darkness. We don't have the power to stand on our own and create light where there is none. But God! He has proven that He can bring light to the darkness, to the world, and to your life. And He has promised that a day is coming when all will be light.

The city does not need the sun or the moon to shine on it, because the glory of God illuminates it, and its lamp is the Lamb. ... Night will be no more; people will not need the light of a lamp or the light of the sun, because the Lord God will give them light, and they will reign forever and ever.

REVELATION 21:23; 22:5

When the darkness that surrounds us feels suffocating, God's Word strengthens our resolve that the darkness will not take away our light. While the world is groaning for the return of Jesus and for order to be restored, we have strength and rescue in Jesus, our Light.

Write John 8:12 below.

Today, take the promises of peace, hope, and redemption with you as you go, and hold them close to your heart. Don't let the rush of Christmas parties and cookie exchanges steal the joy and hope we have in the message of Christ. Even with the darkness all around, we have a real and true hope in our God, who is able to create light amid the darkness.

Take a few minutes to journal a prayer to God, thanking Him for sending light to the darkness. Consider how you can live as a light for others during this season of Advent.

THE DARKNESS INSIDE EACH OF US

by Kelly D. King

First, read Romans 3:21-26.

Mammoth Cave National Park is the longest known cave system on earth, stretching more than four hundred miles under the earth's surface. On a recent visit, I found myself on a tour with more than one hundred people and a trusted guide, who carried a flashlight and the important knowledge of the light system that would direct our steps.

As we reached the deepest point of the cave, the guide gathered our group and explained that he wanted to turn off all sources of light so we could experience total darkness. For a just a few seconds, everything went black. We couldn't even see our own hands in front of our faces. The darkness felt overwhelming. I was grateful when the lights came back on.

Within each of our souls is a darkness even more overwhelming. It's a darkness that can only be overcome by salvation through Christ. That darkness is called sin, and the light that is made available for all of us is found in the arrival of a baby named Jesus, the perfect gift we didn't deserve and couldn't earn.

How would you define *sin*? Read 1 John 3:4-5 for some help.

Replace the words "everyone" and "you" with your name. Does that change the way you understand these verses and understand sin? Describe how.

Revisit Romans 3:21-26. According to this passage, who has sinned and fallen short of God's glory (v. 23)?

This passage may not make your list of favorite familiar Christmas verses, but perhaps it should. Paul's words help us understand our need for Jesus' incarnation. Our sin is why He came!

In the first few chapters of Romans, the apostle Paul vividly outlined the depravity of man and God's judgment. Consider again Genesis 3 when the world was marred by the fall and humankind was infected with sin. By eating of the tree of the knowledge of good and evil, Adam and Eve not only broke their right relationship with God, but their action determined the essential nature of everyone else who has been born. Ever since that first bite of forbidden fruit, "all have sinned and fall short of the glory of God" (Rom. 3:23). Our hearts are darkened because of sin. And because God is holy, sin separates us from Him (Isa. 59:2). Only the One who is without sin, Jesus, could restore our broken relationship with God.

READ ROMANS 3:10-12.

- Who is righteous (v. 10)?

- Who understands and seeks God (v. 11)?

- Who has turned away (v. 12)?

- Who does what is good (v. 12)?

No one is right before God. We are all guilty of sin and its consequences.

These may not be the warm sentiments you like to dwell on at Christmas, but don't lose hope! Paul is about to turn the corner in Romans 3.

Read Romans 3:21. Write down the first two words of this verse.

These two simple words—"But now"—begin a new theme for Paul. These two words may be the greatest turning point in the Book of Romans. They may be the greatest turning point for the human race!

Paul's intentionality from Romans 1:18–3:20 is a reminder that we must understand the past so we can appreciate the present. "But now" becomes a shout for joy when we understand what we have been rescued from. Paul was saying that righteousness has come for everyone! Without the bitter pill of our sin, this truth would not be so sweet. The light and hope of the Advent season lose their impact when we miss the darkness and devastation of our sin.

With this in mind, reread Romans 3:22-26.

The word "redemption" was likely quickly understood by the readers of Paul's day because it was a term of the slave market. Many historians agree that more than half of the population of first-century Rome were slaves.[9] The Gentile audience understood this term because they knew the process of paying a ransom price for freedom. The Jewish audience knew God's law concerning slaves and their own exodus to freedom from the Egyptians. What was new to these audiences was that there was a kind of slavery for all people—sin—that was paid by only one ransom price—the price of Jesus' death on the cross.

See, these *are* Christmas verses! Jesus came as a baby, but He didn't stay that way. He came to pay the ransom required to buy back His children, living in a sin-infected world.

Something changes when we are made right before God. We shift from people walking in darkness to people walking in light.

READ EPHESIANS 5:8.

- What phrase describes the past?

- What phrase describes the present?

- What phrase describes the present and the future?

Though our hearts were once enslaved to darkness, through Christ, we are brought into the light. Because the Holy Spirit dwells in us, we carry the light of Christ in our daily lives. For some, the light might be burning bright. For others, the pull of sin may be causing the light to dim.

READ EPHESIANS 2:1-10.

Maybe today's lesson has brought up some personal questions about your own relationship with God. Have you experienced what it means to turn from darkness to light?

One of the most common experiences of Christmas is the giving of gifts. Christ's birth was the greatest gift offered to humanity. And it truly is a gift; we don't have to earn it. It's a generous gift that came with a great cost—a sacrifice on the cross. You and I have the choice whether to accept the gift of salvation or reject it. We come to faith in Christ not because of our own perfection but through the perfection of Jesus.

Reflect on Ephesians 2:8-9 below:

> For you are saved by grace through faith, and this is not from yourselves; it is God's gift—not from works, so that no one can boast.

If you have received God's gift of salvation, stop and spend a few moments thanking Him for His indescribable gift.

If you aren't sure if you have a relationship with Christ, today can be the day you receive His gift of salvation. You can turn from your own ways to Christ, asking Him to lead your life.

I encourage you to pray a prayer similar to this:

Dear God, I know I am a sinner. I believe Jesus came to earth to provide a way for me to be forgiven of my sins. I accept the gift of salvation that you have offered to me and the promise of eternal life. Thank You for Your forgiveness. For the rest of my life, I choose to follow You.

There's nothing magical about the specific words listed above. The important part is confessing your need for God, asking Him to be in charge of your life. When we turn from our sins and trust Jesus by faith for new hope and eternal salvation, God makes us new! It's a miracle, truly.

If you prayed this prayer, I celebrate with you! I encourage you to seek out a local church and connect with them. You were never designed to follow Christ on your own but with a community of other believers. The church isn't perfect, but they are seeking to follow Christ just like you.

Day 3

JESUS IS THE LIGHT

by Erin Ivey

First, read Isaiah 9:2.

Imagine with me: You wake up to sunlight streaming into your bedroom after you've had the most perfect night of uninterrupted sleep. There's a glorious pot of coffee (or tea, if that's your thing) waiting for you as you start your day with your quiet time with the Lord. You are having the best hair day of your life, and your schedule is full of warm sunshine in the great outdoors and spending time with all your favorite people. Picture a day filled with laughter, connection, and pure radiance.

> Do you have a near-perfect day in your life that you look back on with joy and happiness?

If you're like me, then you immediately think of Cheryl Frasier from *Miss Congeniality*. When she answered the question of what her perfect date would be, she said, "That's a tough one. I would have to say April 25. Because it's not too hot, not too cold; all you need is a light jacket."[10] Well, ladies, I think we can all agree that Cheryl wasn't wrong. That does sound like a perfect day!

Now, picture a day without sunlight. Imagine no warmth and no vitamin D. In one town in Alaska, residents didn't see the sun for sixty-five days.[11] *Sixty-five days.* Only darkness. I can't speak for you, but I know how the lack of sun would make me feel. Tired, confused, a little lost, and desperate for the light.

Beginning in Genesis 1, when God created the world, the Bible references light over two hundred times![12] Why? Because our souls are desperate for it.

Write Isaiah 9:2 below.

In our key verse for today, the light represents Jesus, our living hope. In Isaiah's day, as in ours, people were searching for a rescue from the spiritual darkness that surrounded them.

Have you ever been in a season of darkness? Did you seek rescue?

Spiritually speaking, I've had seasons of hiding in the darkness, trying to avoid the light. But the unique thing about light is that it can't help but illuminate. It can't help but dispel the darkness. That's the nature of light—it always pushes back against darkness.

Sometimes light exposes something we prefer to keep hidden, whether it be something as small as a blemish or something as big as a sin that we've been hiding for so long. Exposure is ultimately a mercy. The burden of carrying our sin is too much for us to bear on our own. When we seek to hide our sin, we find ourselves living in shame and regret, desperately wishing for an escape. Our souls were made to move toward the light, toward the freedom of the exposure of our sin.

Is there something you are trying to keep hidden in the darkness?

In times of hiding, it can be easy to lose sight of the light we have in Jesus. Light = hope, and hope = Jesus. In every season, Jesus is our Source of true light, of true hope.

READ JOHN 8:12.

How did Jesus describe Himself?

God's Word helps us see that the light overpowers darkness every time. The darkness can never extinguish the light of Christ. Never ever.

Write John 1:4-5 below.

How does this description of Jesus give you hope?

The hope and joy of this season is not yours to create. We don't have to task ourselves with making everything perfect. God sent His Son to be our light in this world. He is the beacon of hope our hearts are desperate for. The white lights around our tree, the candles we light on our Advent wreaths, the colored bulbs that adorn the roofs in our neighborhood—these are all reminders that Jesus is the Light of the world. He came to push back against the darkness.

This Christmas season, be a light to the others around you. Show them the light of Christ and the hope He brings to all who know and love Him! This is a special time to not only hold onto these truths but to spread the gospel to those living in darkness.

There is everlasting hope in Christ. We need to hear this every day, and we need to share this message of rescue with everyone around us.

> The sun will no longer be your light by day, and the brightness of the moon will not shine on you. The LORD will be your everlasting light, and your God will be your splendor. Your sun will no longer set, and your moon will not fade; for the LORD will be your everlasting light, and the days of your sorrow will be over.

ISAIAH 60:19-20

Write down Isaiah 60:19-20 and hang it on your bathroom mirror where you can see it each morning and night. Pray this as a reminder that you have everlasting light in the Lord, and thank God for His gift of Jesus to humanity.

LIVING IN LIGHT WHILE WE WAIT

by Joy Allmond

First, read Ephesians 5:6-11.

Darkness can show up in the most unexpected places, even during the hopeful, joyous season of Advent. Perhaps especially during the hopeful, joyous season of Advent.

One of those unexpected places is among loved ones. This is the season many of us gather with the people who knew us "when"—the people who likely knew us before we knew Christ. We love our families of origin, but sometimes they bring out the worst in us. When we're around the people who knew us when we walked in darkness, it's easy to fall back into those dark, old sin patterns—even when we're people of light.

The Letter to the Ephesians was written to a newly-formed family, one united by the blood of Christ, the long-awaited for Emmanuel. And as with any new family, this one was learning how to walk, live, and serve wisely together in the light.

Ephesians 5:6-11 cautions us about our proclivity to veer toward the darkness we were rescued and ransomed from, and instead, urges us as believers, the recipients of eternal hope, to cling to the light.

One of the ways we can fall prey to the darkness is through deception (vv. 6-7). Because our dead sin nature still clings to us, we can be deceived into falling back into our old patterns. We can get a short-lived high from spouting off a snarky comeback. We can get a sense of importance from the surge of pride we allow to swell within our hearts. We can get a false sense of fulfillment when our former idols woo us with empty promises. We can romanticize a past of patterns that only left us defeated.

But we have the power, through the resurrected Jesus, to say no to this deception.

Revisit Ephesians 5:6. Write down Paul's words.

"Let no one deceive you …" This is not a statement of powerlessness. Instead, this proclaims the authority we have in Christ to quash any lies that tell us we are who we once were and try to strong-arm us into reverting back into that person.

Paul then offered another bold suggestion: He reminded us that we should no longer live as the people we were, but that we have a new family identity—an identity that can be clouded by disobedience. It's important to remember we're obedient in response to our acceptance into God's family, not the reverse (Eph. 1: 4-5).

What's your motivation to live as a person of the light? Is it to gain favor with the Lord? You already have His favor and His acceptance. If you're in Christ, you're already part of His family. The reason for our obedience—for casting His light—should be in response to the lavish grace He has poured out on us (Eph. 1:6) and His kindness in saving us.

We live as people of light not just actively, but proactively, combatting the darkness that so desperately wants to reclaim our souls and render us defeated. This means we expose the darkness (Eph. 5:11).

What does it mean to expose something?

To expose the darkness sometimes means we fight for the vulnerable or work to bring justice to people who have suffered at the hands of evil. Other times it means that we, as people of light, live in a way that wages war on the darkness that threatens our own souls.

Write Ephesians 5:11 below.

Sometimes our human vision allows the lines to get blurred between who we used to be and who we are today.

> Can you think of any ways you might be deceived into participating in, rather than fighting against, the darkness?

> Are there any ways you're confusing the old self with the new self?

By simply refusing the odd comfort of living as people we no longer are, we pierce the darkness as we collectively shout with our testimonies, "Emmanuel has come," and because He has come, we have been changed.

Are you prepared to cast the light of Christ during this special—but sometimes awkward and difficult—season? Some of you may be gearing up to have extended time with people who don't nurture your life in Christ or honor the eternal family you're a part of. Others of us are heading into this season with darkness looming over us for other reasons, be it career challenges, financial difficulties, or health fears.

Whatever the case, remember who you are. You are a person who lives in the light. And remember whose you are. You are a child of God. You're a part of an eternal family—a family that pierces the darkness with light in order to point to the One who has come for us.

As we live and walk as people of light, let's not take for granted that our already-but-not-yet-dead flesh still adorns our bodies. Whether you picked up your worldly tendencies through generational transference, by conditioning through years of living apart from Christ, or a little of both, know Jesus did more than come to earth for you; He empowers you to live in the light.

Practice seeking His presence. Pray that your focus will be on what Jesus has done *for* you instead of the damage this world has done *to* you.

Live as a person of light.

JESUS, THE LIGHT OF THE WORLD NOW AND FOREVERMORE

by Amanda Mae Steele

First, read Revelation 22:5-6.

Do you love daydreaming about the bright future ahead? Or do you tend to shrink back for fear of what might happen? Perhaps you prefer to spend your time reminiscing about "the good old days" instead.

Regardless of your opinion on whether the best days are yet to come or the best days have come and gone, the truth about the future is crystal clear in God's Word. Rest assured: you will find even more joy if you're already excited about it, great comfort if you're worried about it, and surprising hope if you're skeptical about it.

In order to fully understand today's key text, we need to make sure we read it in its full context and also understand a few key things about the Book of Revelation. If you're like me, you may find that the book in the back of your Bible can be very intimidating, so let's pause here, and I'd like to pray the same passage Paul wrote to fellow believers over you:

> I pray that the God of our Lord Jesus Christ, the glorious Father, would give you the Spirit of wisdom and revelation in the knowledge of him. I pray that the eyes of your heart may be enlightened so that you may know what is the hope of his calling, what is the wealth of his glorious inheritance in the saints, and what is the immeasurable greatness of his power toward us who believe, according to the mighty working of his strength.

EPHESIANS 1:17-19

Allow me to share a little bit of background. Just as you wouldn't read *The Lion, the Witch and the Wardrobe* as if it were history, we need to understand what type of biblical literature Revelation is and read it that way.

Unlike other books of the Bible that may primarily be just one genre (e.g., history, poetry, law, etc.), there are three genres within Revelation. It contains letters along with prophetic and apocalyptic literature.

> I'm guessing we're all familiar with what a letter is, but let's look up and write the definitions of the following below:
>
> - Apocalyptic
>
> - Prophetic

In a nutshell, in addition to the letters to the seven churches, Revelation is a book that describes the end times and what will happen in the future. As believers in Christ, we don't need to fear the future because all things will be made new (Rev. 21:5). We can eagerly anticipate Christ's second coming, knowing we have an incredible future ahead of us, one so wonderful our minds can't fully comprehend it (1 Cor. 2:9). And with that, let's jump in!

REVISIT REVELATION 22:5-6.

Record the details found in verse 5.

This verse describes the new Jerusalem. What excites you most when you think about our eternal home?

READ REVELATION 21:9–22:6.

As you're reading, pay attention to the vivid imagery John used to describe the holy heavenly city. Write down any descriptors that excite, delight, or intrigue you.

Think about the current world we live in and compare and contrast it with the new Jerusalem described in Revelation 21:22–22:5:

THE WORLD WE LIVE IN	THE NEW JERUSALEM

John's vision in Revelation of the new Jerusalem and the restored garden of Eden (Rev. 22:1-5) is quite fantastic and challenging for our finite brains to comprehend:

- A city of pure gold (21:18).
- The walls of the city bedazzled with gems (21:19-20).
- Pearls as big as city gates (21:21).
- A city with no night and no sun (21:23).

Yet in Revelation 22:6, we receive assurance from God's angel: "These words are faithful and true." We can cling to this promise of a light-filled city in which we will dwell and reign with God as hope for our future.

But what do we do today while our souls are still longing for relief from the darkness, singing:

O come, Thou Dayspring, come and cheer

Our spirits by Thine advent here;

Disperse the gloomy clouds of night,

And death's dark shadows put to flight.

Rejoice! Rejoice! Emmanuel

Shall come to thee, O Israel.[13]

If you have put your faith in Jesus, you can take heart, knowing you don't have to wait for Christ's second coming to experience His light and live by it. Though we still live in a world in which darkness exists, there is good news!

In him was life, and that life was the light of men. That light shines in the darkness, and yet the darkness did not overcome it.

JOHN 1:4-5

If you're skeptical about this fact, I challenge you to try this (carefully!): go into a pitch black room and strike a match (or if you're worried about setting something on fire, just click the home screen on your phone so that it lights up). Even a small amount of light infiltrates every part of darkness.

Light provides illumination, helping us to see the world around us and giving us perspective. We do not need to be overwhelmed by darkness or night because Jesus promises us we will never walk in darkness. As long as we follow Him, He is actively at work illuminating our steps.

How has Jesus been the light of your world?

When Jesus described Himself as the Light of the world (John 8:12), and when John wrote about Jesus as the "light of men" (1:4), the word "light" is the Greek word *phos*—the same light God promises to provide in Revelation 22:5.[14] We can rejoice because Jesus is the Light of the world, which we have access to both here and now and also in the future!

Jesus also calls us to bear His light to the world.

READ MATTHEW 5:14-16.

How are God's children described?

Let us not live in darkness; instead, let's live by and be bearers of His light as we eagerly await the day when there will be no more night, that we may help draw the world to Him.

> In what areas of your life are you experiencing darkness or night in which you need Christ's light now?

> Is there someone in your life who needs Christ's light this season?

> What are you most looking forward to in the future, when you finally are able to fully experience life without tears, death, grief, crying, or pain (Rev. 21:4) with Christ?

Wrap up this week of study, by praying a prayer similar to the one below.

Heavenly Father, thank You for sending us Your Son, Jesus Christ, through whom we have the Holy Spirit to guide us and provide us with the light we need to navigate this life. Thank You for Your Word, which is a lamp to our feet and a light to our path. Help us to wait with patience, hope, and joy for Christ's return, for the day when all things will be made new, when we will be able to experience the fullness of joy in Your presence. Amen.

MAKE SLOW COOKER

Candles

by Larissa Arnault Roach

In John 9:5, Jesus tells us He is the Light of the world. Create slow cooker candles in warm holiday scents to remind yourself each time you burn one that Jesus brings light into your life. He is hope in literal and spiritual darkness.

GATHER

- 4 pounds of soy wax
- 10 (4-ounce) mason jars
- Slow cooker
- Boiling water
- Canning tongs or tongs wrapped with rubber bands*
- Essential oils of your choice
- 10 cotton wicks
- Skewer
- 10 clothes pins

DIRECTIONS

1. Supplies can easily be ordered online. Gather items and get everything set up to begin.

2. Fill each mason jar to the top with wax pieces. Place the jars in the bottom of an empty slow cooker and slowly pour boiling water around the jars until about halfway up the sides, being careful not to get water into the jars. Place the lid on the slow cooker and set the temperature to high.

3. After two hours, the wax will have melted to about half the volume. Add more wax and stir. Place the lid back on the slow cooker and let sit on high for another hour.

4. Once all the wax has melted, carefully remove the jars from the slow cooker with tongs and let sit at room temperature for ten minutes.

   *Note: If you do not have canning tongs, wrap a few rubber bands around each grabbing end of a regular pair of tongs to create a stronger grip.

5. Add a generous amount of essential oils (about forty drops) to each candle.

6. When the wax just starts to set, use a skewer to create a hole in the wax and insert the wicks. To keep each wick upright while the wax cools completely, insert the wick through the hole in the center of a wooden clothespin, then rest it on top of the upper rim of the jar while the wax sets.

7. Let your candles cool for several hours before trimming the wicks and screwing on the lids. Decorate each finished candle with twine and a gift tag.

CANDLELIGHT

Hope

by Michelle Prater Freeman

Winter days can be somber and gloomy. Our hearts can be heavy and dim. But Christmas is a great reminder that Jesus is "the Dayspring from on high" (Luke 1:78, NKJV), and His light shines far beyond any darkness.

A tornado ripped through our city recently. It could've been easy to focus only on the darkness it brought—death, devastation, and a literal blackout for some. But I couldn't avoid seeing all the light that followed: tons of donations, endless lines of volunteers, and evidence of Jesus' love through it all.

We often take light for granted. And thanks to cell phones, we have illumination within reach no matter where we are. But this December, plan a special dinner with your teen and change the rules: no electric lights, no light from devices, candlelight only. Many teens have never experienced a true candlelight dinner! Gather around the kitchen table with some takeout and a half dozen candles. For fun, poke mini marshmallows onto skewers and try roasting them over the candle flames. Don't let dinner end before talking about the way even a single candle still allows you to see whom you're with and what you're eating.

Jesus is that flame for us—whether it's a tragic storm or just a winter day when you're wishing for some sun. He was sent to light our path: "Because of our God's merciful compassion, the dawn from on high will visit us" (Luke 1:78). At Christmastime and all the time, never forget we are children of the light.

A LANTERN

Testimony

by Shelly D. Harris

In the Bible, sin is compared to darkness, and God is described as light. One night in the small town of Bethlehem, our Dayspring—the Light of the world—was born and placed in a small manger. This baby would change the world forever.

Explain that the name Dayspring is a name for Jesus that reminds us He is our hope and light.

READ ISAIAH 9:2 AND LUKE 2:30-32.

Point out that Jesus is the light. In the Gospel of John, Jesus explained to everyone that He is the Light of the world. He came to earth to show us how to have a relationship with God. Jesus pointed everyone from the darkness of sin to the light of God.

DIRECTIONS

Create a lantern to remind everyone that Jesus is our hope and light. Gather a mason jar (or recycle an empty pickle jar); red, yellow, and green tissue paper; a battery-operated tea light; a bottle of decoupage glue; and a paintbrush. Invite kids to tear or cut the tissue paper into small squares. Then help kids use decoupage glue to attach the tissue paper squares all around the jar. After the glue dries, turn on the tea light and place it inside the jar.

Remind everyone that one day Jesus will return and make all things new. Darkness will no longer exist. No one will need a lamp or a flashlight because Jesus will be our light—forever.

Conclude with prayer: *We praise You, Lord, for being our light and our hope. Help us to remember to live in ways that bring You honor and glory. We thank You for defeating sin and death by dying on the cross and rising again. Amen.*

wisdom

O COME, THOU WISDOM

by Elizabeth Hyndman

At first, this verse seems a bit mysterious. "O come, Thou Wisdom from on high, and order all things, far and nigh; to us the path of knowledge show, and cause us in her ways to go."[15]

Before Jesus came to earth as Emmanuel, God's people felt their deep need for wisdom. They lived in a time when they hadn't heard from God in hundreds of years. They wanted knowledge of Him. They craved wisdom.

Don't we crave wisdom too? We want to know the best way to navigate the many challenges of life. We need guidance for the ups and downs of our relationships. We desire to know God and how to please Him. We're uncomfortable not knowing. We're hungry to know information and apply it well (i.e., be wise) as evidenced by our obsessive searching for information. We clearly don't like dwelling in the chaos of ignorance.

We also desire order. We don't like living in uncertainty. Yet our world is a disordered, uncertain place. We don't understand why things happen the way they do. We cannot know what will happen. *Will this natural disaster destroy the lives of those*

I love? Will this person forgive me? Will this person keep a promise? Will the future I envision for myself become a reality? We do not easily trust what we do not know.

Into this, we ask wisdom to come. To order things. To illuminate our paths. We need Jesus to help us to walk in wisdom while we anticipate the day when we will know God fully.

The words of this ancient Christmas hymn are a prayer and a statement of faith. We are asking the Lord to give us wisdom and expressing our trust that He is our wise Father, the one who makes the crooked paths of life run straight.

Lead everyone to write down a definition for *wisdom* and then share what they wrote with the group.

Read 1 Kings 3:7-9. How would you state Solomon's prayer in your own words?

Read 1 Kings 3:1-14. Why do you think it pleases the Lord when we seek wisdom?

Consider the wise men recorded as part of the Christmas story in Matthew 2:1-2. How did wisdom lead them to respond to Jesus? How can we follow their example?

Share areas of your life in which you are seeking the Lord's wisdom this Advent season.

WISE IN OUR OWN EYES

by Sarah H. Doss

First, read Proverbs 3:7.

By nature, I'm a problem solver. Most of the time this skill comes in handy, but every now and then calling myself a problem solver can be a nice way of justifying some anxious tendencies that run deeply through my heart and mind.

Here's usually how this unfolds: I encounter some sort of challenge or obstacle, and I turn the issue over and over in my mind. My brain runs on autopilot. I think if I can just let the situation simmer, I'll see every angle of the issue; I'll run through possible solutions and eventually my brain will magically produce a genius solution. Then I'll implement the fix, and *voila!* Everyone can move on. Piece of cake. Right? Wrong.

Honestly, this approach only works out on very rare occasions. In large part, most of the issues that make their way into my heart and mind are very complex—things I couldn't understand or deconstruct if I wanted to—in a nutshell, these are not quick fixes. So my overthinking-the-problem approach ends up leaving me stressed and without solutions. I think I'm up to the challenge and I know what's best, but, in truth, the dilemma is often beyond my abilities.

The Bible tells me that I'm not the only one who has struggled with this particular proclivity.

> **Pick three of the passages from the following list. In the chart on the next page, describe who is acting, what they considered wisdom, and what God said was wisdom.**
>
> Genesis 3:1-19 • Genesis 11:1-9 • Joshua 7:10-26 • 2 Samuel 11
> • John 2:13-17 • John 9:1-7

PERSON ACTING	MAN'S WISDOM	GOD'S WISDOM

We see in these examples folks who either ignored God's direction and thought they knew better, or people who, though well-intentioned, bungled things by acting according to man-made wisdom. Over and over again the Bible encourages us to choose God's way over our own and to admit that we don't have all of the answers. Through His Word, God reminds us to come to Him with our questions because He is the source of wisdom. Walking in line with God's ways will lead to life and joy for us. R. C. Sproul says, "Wisdom has to do with the practical matter of learning how to live a life that is pleasing to God."[16]

If wisdom is the path to joy and a life that pleases God, who wouldn't want it? Why do we seem to struggle so much to come in line with God's ways? There are a million reasons why I choose to go my own way, to bypass God's guidance in favor of what seems right, convenient, or fun to me at the time.

Think back over the past month. Below, describe a situation in which you acted in your own wisdom, intentionally or unintentionally, and realized you weren't following the wisdom of God.

Can you trace the root of your actions? Why do you think you acted the way you did?

What might your actions be revealing about what you believe? About God? About yourself? Are there any threads of unbelief or distrust in your heart that lead you to try to take control? Explain below. Feel free to also take some time here to pray and ask God to reveal any sin that might need to be confessed. Tell Him about any wounds or places of hurt that may have surfaced here.

If the activity above helped you identify a place of unbelief or hurt, take a moment to track down a Bible passage that speaks truth to the issue you're facing. (For example, if I'm struggling to believe that God will be kind to me amidst hardship, I might write Psalm 56:9b-11a below: "This I know: God is for me. In God, whose word I praise, in the LORD, whose word I praise, in God I trust; I will not be afraid.")

READ JOB 28.

Look at verses 1-11. What does this section of the text really focus on? Sum up the concepts in a sentence or two.

Now hone in on verses 12-22. Where does the focus of the text shift? What do you notice about the difference in tone?

Finally, reread verses 23-28. What do you think these verses are saying about God's character and His actions?

Write verse 28 below.

The Book of Job recounts the story of a righteous man who had served God faithfully for years and was suddenly forced to endure hardship after hardship. This book relays a head-scratching scenario that makes little sense to our human minds. Job sows in faithfulness, yet he reaps what seems like punishment. In the midst of Job's wrestlings, we find this beautiful chapter on the origin of wisdom.

This passage tells us that God has taught men how to find many hidden and very valuable things—how to mine gold and precious jewels from the earth, how to make bread from the wheat we harvest. But in verse 12, man, whom we've seen to be so resourceful, runs into a snag. He can't seem to unearth wisdom. He searches in all the usual hidden places, but he can't find wisdom. Wisdom can't be bargained for or bought with silver and gold. It's more valuable than precious things on earth. So, what's the deal? Where are wisdom and understanding? Turns out, they are with God. *He made wisdom; only He knows where to find it.*

In God's kindness, He's clued us in: "The fear of the Lord—that is wisdom. And to turn from evil is understanding" (Job 28:28).

What do you think "the fear of the Lord" means?

The fear of the Lord is a reverence and respect of who He is. This fear is not the same as being afraid of God; instead, it's an acknowledgement of how much higher He is than we are, how much kinder and steadier, and that He is infinitely more powerful and gracious than we could ever be.

Many see the Book of Job as the answer to the question of why God allows suffering in the lives of His children. We are not met with easy answers. Instead, we are met with a consistently kind refrain, pointing us to God as the source of all wisdom, all comfort, all hope, purpose, and joy. In his suffering, Job is met with the promise of God's presence. In our struggles to act wisely and solve the problems we face on this earth, we're not left alone to let the what-ifs swirl endlessly. We're graciously held by a Father who grants wisdom to those who ask Him (Jas. 1:5); He's promised to help us search it out. (More on that tomorrow.)

As we close today, take a moment to consider how you can worship God in this Advent season for His infinite wisdom in sending Jesus as a baby to save us—something that made no sense to man's finite mind at the time, but indeed has brought us great tidings of comfort and joy.

How does seeing God's faithfulness in this situation, one that didn't seem wise in man's eyes, inform the way you face hard situations in your life now? How does it help you trust Him more?

GOD IS WISDOM

by Ravin McKelvy

𝕱𝖎𝖗𝖘𝖙, 𝖗𝖊𝖆𝖉 𝕽𝖔𝖒𝖆𝖓𝖘 𝟙𝟙:𝟛𝟛-𝟛𝟞.

Our triune God of paradoxes—both three and one.

Infinitely self-giving in His love.

This is the God who confounds us

by the depth of the riches of His wisdom and knowledge.

Wisdom and knowledge that are not simply competent,

but an experienced and lived reality—

an intimate understanding that is gained through relationship.

Our God who does not only have wisdom or give wisdom,

but who is, Himself, wisdom.

It is from Him and through Him and to Him that all things belong.

What is the first thing that comes to mind when you think of the wisdom of God?

READ PSALM 139:1-18.

In Psalm 139, David wrote about the infinite knowledge and presence of God. Poetically, he proclaimed that God knows when he sits down, when he travels, and even his thoughts before they're formed. But as we read through this passage, we are clued in to something intrinsically connected to God's wisdom. The psalmist's deep proclamation of God's wisdom opens the curtain to intimacy. We see that God does not simply search us and know us, but that He understands us. He did not only see us when we were formless, but He also gave us form as He knitted us in our mother's womb. He does not remember us only on occasion but thinks of us so often that His thoughts outnumber every grain of sand. It is from Him that we receive our being and from His wisdom that we are sustained.

But here is where the wisdom of God becomes even more astonishing. Having a perfect and complete knowledge of us, He has opened Himself so that He may also be known by us. God, who is wisdom, gives us wisdom by giving of Himself. God gave His Son so that He who is invisible and has never been seen could be seen and made known (John 1:18; Col. 1:15). And God gave us His Spirit to open our eyes so that we may know and understand that Scripture speaks of Him (John 16:13-16). It is from God that we receive wisdom.

Take some time now to write a prayer, asking God to give you wisdom so that you may know Him more intimately.

READ PROVERBS 8:27-31.

Throughout Proverbs we see references to God creating through wisdom. In Proverbs 8, wisdom is said to have been with God throughout creation, like "a skilled craftsman beside him" (v. 30). It was through God's wisdom that everything came into being. And in these verses we also see that it is through wisdom that God delights in His creation.

Here we see that God not only knows us intimately and makes Himself known to us, but that as He knows, He also delights. This is a profound truth for us to ponder on—that the God who is wisdom, the God who knows us to the depth of our being, delights in us.

Think of a couple welcoming their newborn child. As they hold their baby for the first time, they are filled with the delight of their child. This child, who is completely dependent on his parents and unable to provide anything for them, is delighted in, truly treasured. The parents delight in their child not because he's done anything but because of who he is—their child, who has come through their union.

How often do we forget that we are already delighted in? It can be so easy for us to get caught up trying to be or do something to earn God's delight that we forget He has delighted in us since before we could do anything. It is through His wisdom that we were created, and, because we are His creation, we are delighted in.

In what ways do you try to earn God's delight?

What would it look like to let go of those things and rest in the delight of the Lord simply because you are His child?

REREAD ROMANS 11:33-36.

Let's circle back to our original passage. Thus far in the Book of Romans, Paul has addressed many things, spending a large portion of time on humankind's rejection of God. Like a lawyer building a case, Paul presented evidence of God's righteousness and man's unrighteousness. And just as it seems that condemnation will be the final sentencing, Paul proclaimed that we are justified in Christ. He unraveled the plan that God has had from the beginning. The plan to be merciful on all who believe in His Son by grafting them into His family. The plan in which the lost are called to Him and the rejected belong to Him.

It is because God's wisdom is intimate and sees with delighting eyes that He can be merciful. God knows and understands the depth of sin in us—it is not in ignorance that He delights in His creation. And it is not in ignorance that He has mercy either. It is in His profound merciful wisdom that He looks upon those who have faith in Him and sees the righteousness of His Son.

It makes sense why, in light of this reality, Paul paused to write a hymn of praise. What other response can we have to the beauty of God's intimate, delighting, merciful wisdom?

In this season of Advent, we worship the God who is wisdom. We wait expectantly, proclaiming that it is from Him and through Him and to Him we belong and have our being. And we continually ponder on the depth of the riches of God's wisdom.

> As you reflect on the beauty that God is wisdom, write your own poem in response to what you've read today.

Day 3

JESUS IS THE WISDOM OF GOD

by W. Diane Braden

First, read Matthew 1:18-25.

Picture a world in turmoil. Mary, a young and unmarried girl, was chosen to carry our salvation within her. Joseph, a carpenter, was chosen to raise the cornerstone, the rock of our salvation. Envision visitations by the angel of the Lord to both Mary and Joseph. These messages revealed God's masterful plan, carried out through conception by the Holy Spirit, which brought forth Jesus, the Messiah. Wisdom permeates each part of the Trinity collectively and individually.

All was a divine plan for laying the foundation for God's promise to come to pass.

In Matthew 1:18-25 we are given a glimpse of a beautiful picture of unconditional love. We may never be able to fully comprehend this in our lifetime, but in heaven we will see it all so clearly. Jesus is the wisdom of God in the flesh. As He dwelt on earth among us, He gave of Himself and taught that same wisdom to all who would hear Him.

The Gospel writer reveals this clearly in John 1:14:

> The Word became flesh and dwelt among us. We observed his glory, the glory as the one and only Son from the Father, full of grace and truth.

First Corinthians 1:30 is a verse you may not see written in scripted foil letters on Christmas cards, yet it too speaks to the wonder of this season:

> It is from him that you are in Christ Jesus, who became wisdom from God for us—our righteousness, sanctification, and redemption.

When the Word became flesh, He put the love of God on full display. He showcased God's wisdom. In wisdom, God sent His Son as a ransom to save us. In wisdom, He made a way for us to turn away from death and toward eternal life. Matthew Henry writes, "There is a fulness of wisdom in him, as he has perfectly revealed the will of God to mankind. ... The treasures of wisdom are hidden not from us, but for us, in Christ."[17] The divine plan of salvation could only be conceived through God's infinite wisdom manifested in Christ.

> Have you ever wondered why God would send His only Son to save you? Based on what we've learned so far about wisdom, why do you think He did?

READ GALATIANS 3:13-14.

> What do these verses say is the purpose of Christ's sacrifice? What does that mean for us today?

It is only through the grace of God that we are redeemed. "Redeemed" in verse 13 is *exagorazo* in Greek and means "to buy up, i.e. ransom; figuratively, to rescue from loss (improve opportunity)."[18] We were bought with a price, but how was this masterful plan orchestrated? Through godly wisdom that transcends our earthly perspective.

READ 1 CORINTHIANS 1:18-25.

God presented Christ on earth as the representative of His wisdom, revealing His divine plan. This plan, in which the power and wisdom of God manifested itself, provided unrelenting sacrificial love in its truest form. Consider again verse 24:

> Yet to those who are called, both Jews and Greeks, Christ is the power of God and the wisdom of God.

Human wisdom cannot lead to salvation. All our plans to save ourselves from our sin fall woefully short of the holiness of God. None of us would have chosen an unwed mother to birth the Savior, a blue-collar father to raise Him, and a cross to be the bridge to our redemption. And yet Jesus is proof that God's wisdom is far greater than human wisdom, because even "God's foolishness is wiser than human wisdom, and God's weakness is stronger than human strength" (v. 25).

Jesus holds the world together. But from a limited earthly perspective, do you think trusting in Jesus ever appears to be "foolish" to those who don't know Him? How is wisdom used when we trust in Jesus?

From the babe in the manger to the man on the cross, Jesus exemplifies the truest form of wisdom. God's love sent His Son to declare us righteous and cover all our sins, washing us white as snow through the cleansing of Jesus' shed blood. God gave assurance of this by providing a great Mediator—Jesus! In wisdom, Jesus came down and took on life as a servant for our salvation and redemption.

Jesus came down and revealed God to humankind, and once He finished His work and returned to glory, He united humanity to God. What a beautiful truth to ponder this Christmas! Through the wisdom of God, we are free indeed.

If you have not accepted Jesus Christ as your Lord and Savior, the redemptive work of the cross is for you as well. Admit your need for Him. Believe He is who He claims to be, and confess your sin and need for a Savior.

LIVING WISELY

by Valerie Hancock

First, read James 3:17.

The Advent season brings with it a deep sense of closeness and generosity among people, even in the midst of the hustle and bustle. We recognize that celebrating the birth of Christ is a sacred time with many opportunities to share the joy of the season and the hope of the world with family and friends and even strangers.

Jesus brought us many gifts when He came to earth, among them love, joy, peace, compassion, salvation, and wisdom. He is the tangible expression of God's wisdom here on earth. What an amazing gift to share and celebrate at Christmas and all year long.

Wisdom is more than knowing; it's knowing *and* doing what is right. Wisdom is the ability to apply what we know to be good and true and beneficial to our lives. The Lord is our source of all true knowledge and infinite wisdom. When we seek to know Him and understand things from His perspective, we will have the mind of Christ because of the Holy Spirit living in us. God gives us wisdom; therefore, we can be confident when we face adversity.

READ PROVERBS 2:6-8.

According to this passage, why does God give us wisdom?

Together, let's consider what it looks like to live out the wisdom God so graciously gives us through His Word and His presence in our lives.

READ PROVERBS 3:5-8.

Meditate on what this passage means. Write down any observations or questions that come to mind.

We often make split-second decisions based on a gut feeling. We know ourselves, right? So we decide, act, and move on. But let's be honest. We can't always trust our gut. Sometimes it's operating out of fear of letting someone down or doing what we think others expect of us. This is especially true during the holiday season when we are navigating Christmas parties, school events, family celebrations, shopping, and church commitments.

When we allow stress and pressure from the world to impact our decision making, we aren't trusting God with every part of our lives as He asks us to do. When we rely solely on our feelings about what we should do or say, we are not honoring His lordship in our lives.

So pause a moment before you answer that text or respond to that email. Give yourself a day or two to prayerfully consider a new commitment or a request made by a friend or spouse or child. Maybe your gut decisions usually turn out fine. But what if you could make the best possible decision in light of God's direction and His desire for your life? Take the time you need to read God's Word and connect the knowledge of what it says with the action of doing what is right. Pray and ask God for His direction. Consult God first. Not your gut.

In this passage from Proverbs, King Solomon also instructed us to fear the Lord, not to avoid some kind of punishment from Him, but to honor and respect Him, knowing He will give us the strength and guidance we need to avoid a path we shouldn't take. As our heavenly Father, He loves and cares for us beyond what we can comprehend. He wants to show us how to live with purpose and wisdom. To fear Him is to submit to Him in every area of our lives and allow Him to guide our path, recognizing that His ways are beyond what we can understand. God wants our commitment to Him to be undivided because He knows and truly wants what's best for us.

Jot down a few decisions you need to make in the week ahead.

How will you approach these decisions? How will you trust God more and yourself less?

Consider committing Proverbs 3:5-8 to memory this month.

READ 1 CORINTHIANS 3:18-19.

In this passage, Paul wasn't telling the Corinthian believers to neglect the pursuit of knowledge. He was warning them not to put faith in the wisdom of those around them. The Corinthians were boasting about the wisdom of their leaders and teachers, and in their arrogance they were valuing the (wrong) messenger more than the message.

How often do we turn to the latest self-help book or podcast or social media post for insight into what we're going through? Those things aren't necessarily bad for us, unless we don't process what they tell us through the lens of Scripture and the Holy Spirit working in our lives. God's wisdom is far higher and more reliable than any wisdom we could find in a book or on a screen.

Most likely you know someone who seems to possess an unusual capacity to apply God's truth to any situation. Maybe you are in awe of this person. Maybe you're a bit annoyed at times (because you're secretly envious). This person also seems to know the right Bible verse to suggest or the most fitting prayer to pray. The reality is that wisdom is not a superpower. Each of us who knows the living God has the ability to study God's Word and apply it to our lives so we can make wise decisions.

We read in 1 Corinthians 2:16 that we have the mind of Christ because of the work of the Holy Spirit in our lives. This means we approach life from Jesus' point of view, learning to value what He values and think how He thinks. With the mind of Christ we have the opportunity to truly live our lives with humility, compassion, and dependence on God—all attributes that contribute to growing in wisdom.

On the next page are some steps you can take to actively pursue growing in wisdom and align your life to know God in a deeper way.

1. Read God's Word faithfully.

There's a direct correlation between faithful Bible reading and wise living. Find a plan and method that works for you. Focus on quality over quantity, especially in this Advent season, ensuring the words take root in your mind and heart.

2. Talk to God regularly.

Pray as you go about your day. Pray in the early morning and as your day is winding down. Ask God to help you grow in understanding and wisdom. Ask the Holy Spirit to give you supernatural insight and perspective as you read the Bible, attend Bible study, and hear the teaching at your church each week.

3. Get to know the wise.

Surround yourself with people who are known for being wise. Those who possess great wisdom are often peaceful, thoughtful people. Observe their interactions with others; ask them how they connect with God. When they speak, listen to them, because they typically don't mince words or share their insight without considering its value.

4. Live it out.

In Proverbs, there is a chapter corresponding to every day of the month of December. Turn to the chapter in Proverbs that corresponds with today's date. Read until you find one nugget of wisdom that resonates with you today.

How can you apply these steps to your life during this Christmas season?

Pray, thanking God for giving you His wisdom—wisdom that is pure, peace-loving, and gentle (Jas. 3:17).

WISDOM IN THE WAITING

by Ellen Wildman

First, read 1 Corinthians 13:9-13.

A few times a week, I kneel down next to my hot oven in my warm kitchen and watch sourdough bread crack, rise, and bubble in the sizzling cast iron skillet. As I wipe my doughy hands clean, I sigh with contentment.

About a year ago, I became a sourdough bread baker. It began with the gift of a starter and, with a lot of trial and error, has blossomed into baking creations like bread bowls, dinner rolls, pizza, and cinnamon rolls. Sourdough baking has not only taught me patience, but I have also learned that there is joy in the process—in weighing ingredients, mixing and molding dough, shaping loaves—and not just in the final product. There's always another method to learn, another flour to try, another recipe to experiment with. When I pull out a gooey pan of cinnamon rolls and slather them with homemade buttercream, placing them on a table like the prize winning Thanksgiving turkey, and see my friends' faces light up, the strenuous learning process is always worth it.

> When have you experienced a worthwhile and helpful learning process?

Today's passage comes from 1 Corinthians. Paul wrote to the Corinthian believers to both admonish and encourage them as they worked through various issues in their church. Paul penned these words to remind Christians that they will always belong to the Lord and that their identity can be found in Him. The passage today in particular reminds believers of the already/not yet kingdom tension we live in as we pursue Christ.

Are you familiar with the concept of the already/not yet as it relates to the kingdom of God? Describe it below.

REREAD 1 CORINTHIANS 13:9-13.

We feel the tension that Paul described. We are actively taking part in the kingdom of God here on earth, but, at the same time, this kingdom will not be fully revealed to us or experienced by us until Christ's return. This is the wrestling of the already/not yet life of a Christian. This tension finds its home as we individually mature in Christ. Our pursuit of wisdom and faith deepens this pull to heaven, reminding us that we were not made for this place. Just as I become a better baker the more I practice and the more I bake, we grow up in the faith by patiently studying the Word, asking questions of our community, and developing a deeper prayer life. This is how we "put aside childish things" (v. 11). Our pursuit of godly wisdom looks a lot like our pursuit of Jesus Himself.

Name one way you are actively developing and deepening your faith.

In verse 12, Paul reminded us that our current view of the kingdom of God is only partial. Beautiful? Yes. Life-changing? Yes. Transformative? Yes. But until Christ returns and we are with Him in glory, His fullness will not be revealed. Now we know in part, but then we will know fully and be fully known. Our partial perception of Christ will be made complete in eternity, where we will know Him face to face. In the meantime, we can study and mature in our relationship with Him in order to know Him more fully. While we will never fully know Him in this life, growing in Christian wisdom gives us a deeper understanding of God and fuller glimpses of the wisdom of heaven.

What does being fully known by Christ mean to you? How does this make you feel?

Many aspects of church life will cease at the end of this current age, but love never will. As part of the already/not yet state we find ourselves in, we can currently experience the eternal power of Christ's faith, hope, and love within us now. Our faith and hope will be fulfilled in eternity when we are with Christ, but love will remain forever.

> Can you recall a time when you felt God's love most? How would you describe that experience to someone else?

When I first tied up my apron strings and purchased a stack of sourdough baking books, I felt overwhelmed—it hit me like a tidal wave. There were so many steps, instructions, and tools to consult. Only with diligent practice, patience, and care did I battle this stress and come out the other side excited and rewarded with knowledge (and lots of carb-laden treats).

In the same way, our pursuit of Christ matures, refines, and develops us. We pursue God knowing that we are lacking, knowing that we need more of Jesus. As wisdom and knowledge grow, our picture of Him becomes clearer and fuller. As we wade through the tension of the already/not yet, Christ will meet us every time. There is always more of Him, and there is always a deeper knowledge of Him to be found.

We can rest in the fact that while we have much to learn, we can look forward to the day when we will know and be fully known, face-to-face with our Creator. Love was there at the beginning, and love will be there evermore. "Love never ends" (v. 8).

> List a few ways you would like to pursue Christ in order to see Him more clearly.

> How have you seen Jesus be wisdom in your own life?

NOTES

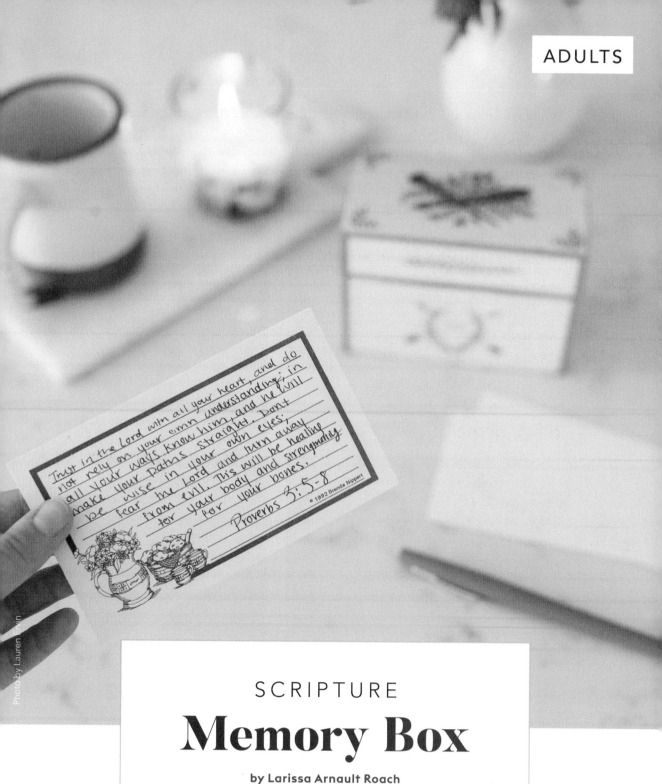

Trust in the Lord with all your heart, and do not rely on your own understanding; in all your ways know him, and he will make your paths straight. Don't be wise in your own eyes; fear the Lord and turn away from evil. This will be healing for your body and strengthening for your bones.
Proverbs 3:5-8

® 1992 Brenda Nippert

SCRIPTURE

Memory Box

by Larissa Arnault Roach

What we think of as wisdom is often not God's wisdom. His ways are not our ways (Isa. 55:8-9). But if we commit God's Word to our hearts and minds, that is a good step toward wise living. Colossians 3:16 encourages us, "Let the word of Christ dwell richly among you, in all wisdom teaching and admonishing one another through psalms, hymns, and spiritual songs, singing to God with gratitude in your hearts."

The following Scripture memorization system helps you review Scripture daily, weekly, and monthly.

GATHER

- Old recipe box
- Cardstock
- Scissors
- Index cards
- Favorite pen

DIRECTIONS

1. Find an old recipe box tall enough to accommodate raised tabs. Print tabbed dividers on heavy cardstock and cut out. Or buy some recipe dividers and create your own labels.

2. Arrange the Scripture memory dividers inside this way:

> 1 "Daily" divider (new verse to review daily)
>
> 1 "Weekly" divider (review every week)
>
> 1 "Monthly" divider (review once a month)

The Daily verse is repeated most often. As you memorize each verse, you review it less and less, and it makes its way to the back of the box.

3. Write down any verses you already know by heart onto 4x6 index cards and evenly distribute them behind the dividers. If you don't know any yet, that's OK!

4. To begin, put one new verse behind the Daily divider. Place other verses you want to memorize in front of the Daily divider. Work on memorizing one verse a week. (In the beginning, you may not have any verses in the Weekly or Monthly slots, but they'll fill in.)

Eventually, you will review three verses by saying one verse behind each of the three dividers.

Keep in mind that only the Daily verse is a new one that you are memorizing; all the others are review.

5. Once a week, or when you're confident in your knowledge of the new verse behind the Daily divider, write the date on the back of the card and advance it by replacing the oldest Weekly card (use past dates as a reference if needed). The

replaced Weekly card goes behind the oldest Monthly card. Then put a new card behind the Daily divider, and you're ready to start your next verse! This repetition will help you hide them in your heart.

Once a week, review the verses behind your Weekly divider, and once a month, review the verses behind your Monthly divider. It might help to think through a routine—for example, every Sunday you review the verses behind your Weekly divider and review the verses behind your Monthly divider the first of each month—whatever works for you!

By the end of the year, think of how many verses you'll have learned![19]

WISDOM ON THE
Small Screen

by Michelle Prater Freeman

I'm in the middle of raising teenagers, and if I asked them to define true wisdom, they'd probably refer to an intelligent friend's perfect ACT score or GPA. But this December, I'd like to give them another definition of wisdom, one God sent to us on the very first Christmas.

There's a whole lot of foolishness in this world, ranging from silly to outright dangerous. Cultural examples are everywhere: plumping our lips to look like celebrities, cheating our way into college, and so forth. But it seems harder to find examples of wisdom or understand where true wisdom comes from.

Scripture gives us the answer: in Christ, "all the treasures of wisdom and knowledge" are hidden (Col. 2:3). When we know Jesus, we share in His wisdom, and His wisdom is often the opposite of what our world considers wise. But how do we get our teens to recognize the difference?

One fun way to start a conversation about foolishness versus wisdom might be a night of watching some silly comedy together with your teen. Try slapstick from an old *The Three Stooges* episode. Or vintage *America's Funniest Home Videos* clips (grown-ups really need to stay off playground equipment). Or watch the now classic *Home Alone*, but try to beat each other at calling out all the foolish choices.

When you're done watching the movie, chat with your teen about more serious, biblical examples of foolishness, such as the people building the Tower of Babel or David pursuing Bathsheba. Try talking about the limits of human intelligence. Then read through Job 28, in which the writer searches high and low to find true wisdom. It's not found in mines full of jewels, in ocean depths, or in this world's riches. It's found in the fear of the Lord ... in Jesus, the source of true wisdom sent to us long ago. Knowing Him makes everything else foolish in comparison and makes Advent even sweeter.

WISDOM THAT
Glitters

by Shelly D. Harris

Our broken world is constantly searching for wisdom in the wrong places. God has given us His wisdom through Jesus. To live wisely, we must seek Jesus and rely on God's wisdom instead of our own.

Read 1 Corinthians 1:24. Explain that Jesus is the wisdom of God. God has given us wisdom through Jesus and through the Word. We must believe in Jesus and read God's Word to gain the wisdom He offers to us.

DIRECTIONS

Gather six large craft sticks and a six-inch piece of ribbon for each family member. Use a hot glue gun to glue two of the craft sticks together to form an X-shape. Glue the other craft stick across the middle of the X-shaped sticks to form a six-pointed star shape ornament. Hot glue a small loop of ribbon to the back of the star so kids can display their stars when finished.

Help kids print with a fine tip marker one word of the phrase "Jesus is the wisdom of God" on each craft stick end, working in a circle so the phrase is in order. Distribute glitter, glue, glitter glue, and foam stickers for everyone to decorate their stars.

As everyone decorates, read some Bible verses about wisdom.

Here are some suggested verses: Proverbs 2:6-8; Proverbs 3:5-6; James 3:17.

Conclude with prayer: *We praise You, Lord, for the gift of Your Son, Jesus. We praise You for being all-wise and ask that You help us seek Your wisdom each day. Amen.*

desire of nations

O COME, DESIRE OF NATIONS

by Elizabeth Hyndman

"Why can't we all just get along?"

It's a common question uttered in households with multiple siblings, in classrooms, in friend groups, and on the Internet. We have a tendency toward envy, strife, and quarrels, don't we?

Perhaps that's why the fourth verse of our carol sings, "O come, Desire of nations, bind all peoples in one heart and mind. Bid envy, strife, and quarrels cease; fill the whole world with heaven's peace."[20]

In the world before Jesus, Cain killed Abel, Sarah banished Hagar and Ishmael from her home, Joseph's brothers sold him, Pharaoh kept the Israelites as slaves, Saul chased after David, kingdoms split, and people groups developed prejudices. Envy, strife, quarrels ...

Into this world came peace—the One who said, "Blessed are the peacemakers" (Matt. 5:9); "Love your enemies" (Matt. 5:44); and "Love ... your neighbor as yourself" (Luke 10:27). In Luke 10, Jesus answered the expert in the Law's question,

"And who is my neighbor?" (v. 29) with a challenge to show mercy toward even those who are outsiders.

Jesus came to bring peace to the world. Through Emmanuel, our enemies become our neighbors, and the nations become our brothers and sisters as we are united in Christ.

One day we will worship Christ together, our hearts and minds as one. We anticipate the day the Desire of nations will come again, and we will live at peace forevermore.

Ask if anyone in your group has experienced Christmas in another country or culture. Encourage them to share their experiences.

How does it encourage your heart to know that Christmas is celebrated globally in almost every culture?

The holiday season can draw attention to painful fractures within relationships. Take time to pray together for opportunities to share the gospel and extend grace to family members and friends who can be hard to love.

Read Revelation 7:9-17 together. Describe what you think it will be like when all of Christ's followers from every nation are united. What excites the members of your group most about this promised moment?

Take the time to confess to each other relationships where you have caused strife or responded with envy or bitterness. Pray for forgiveness together.

IN THIS WORLD THERE ARE QUARRELS AND STRIFE

by Catherine Inman

𝔉irst, read 𝔊enesis 12:1-9.

This passage contains the Abrahamic covenant. It reveals God's promise to bless Abram, his offspring, and all nations through him. This is the beginning of the promise that would eventually find its fulfillment in Jesus, the promise that brought unity to the world.

READ GENESIS 11:26-32.

We are first introduced to Abram in Genesis 11. In just a few short verses, we learn about Abram's father, his wife, and a nugget of biographical information that was key to Abram's story ... and to the gospel story.

What does verse 30 reveal?

The chapters that follow record God calling Abram to leave everything he knew, everything that was familiar, and go to a new land. Though there was no baby on the way, God asked Abram to lead his family into the unknown with the promise that his offspring would be as numerous as the stars (Gen. 22:17).

Imagine the fear and anxiety that must have weighed on Abram. While he was walking down a path that looked hopeless (infertility), God asked him to trust Him.

Is there isolating pain that you are carrying like Abram?

Is money tight? Does it feel like your family is slowly falling apart? Has God asked you to cling to Him, and you just don't know if you can do it anymore?

> **Write down a few reasons why it is hard to trust God in the midst of the unknown.**

I'm so grateful Abram's story is recorded in the pages of Scripture. There it is, in black and white—Abram obeyed. No questions. No mumbling. No time to throw his Instagram® followers a poll to see if he was making the best choice. God spoke, and Abram listened and obeyed. Abram was human. He likely experienced emotional ups and downs, yet he made the choice to believe that God would keep His promise, no matter how impossible it seemed.

> **In a world that tells you to "trust your gut" and "follow your heart," what truths do you cling to? Write down a few Bible verses that keep your feet on solid ground when the world seems to be crumbling around you.**

> **Review Genesis 12:3. Write it below.**

As part of His covenant with Abram, God promised to bless him and bless all the people on earth through him. He also promised to curse those who cursed him. *Pause.* God made this statement in an otherwise positive promise because He knew that Abram would surely encounter quarrels, strife, and discord. Don't we all?

Abram would face people who disagreed with him. There would be times when his own actions would cause pain for himself, and other times when the world around him would bring the pain. And God promised to take care of all of it.

Discord has been a part of the human experience since Adam and Eve sinned in the garden of Eden. Listed below are a few Old Testament accounts that illustrate this reality. Pick two and write down the correlation from these accounts to present day.

	OLD TESTAMENT	PRESENT DAY
Hagar and Ishmael (Gen. 16)		
Sodom and Gomorrah (Gen. 19)		
Jacob and Esau (Gen. 27)		
Rachel and Leah (Gen. 29–30)		

Eventually, the Lord opened Sarai's womb, and she gave birth to a son, Isaac. Isaac fathered Jacob. Jacob fathered twelve sons who became the heads of the twelve tribes of Israel. From the tribe of Judah came David, and from David's line came the Savior whose birth we celebrate in this season—Jesus. Jesus is the ultimate fulfillment of the promise God made to Abram. Truly, through Jesus all the nations of the world have been blessed. In Jesus we find the hope-filled answer to the quarrels and strife of this world.

READ JOHN 16:33.

What declaration did Jesus make in this verse?

Abram faithfully trusted God in the midst of difficult trials and heavy sorrows, and we are called to trust God in our own trials and sorrow. This side of heaven, we live in the known reality that we will have suffering in this world, including envy and strife. Yet, like Abram, we can continue to worship and obey the Lord because we trust that He will keep His promises. He has promised us a home with Him where human strife will cease.

As you think about the sweet promises of God, those made to Abram and those made to you, thank the Lord for them. Testify to those around you, and let them see Him at work in you. Praise Him for caring about the smallest details of your life, including being faithful to keep His Word in a world that longs for unity and peace.

> **Conclude today's study by writing out some of your favorite promises from Scripture and pausing to thank God that He always keeps His promises.**

PEACE IN THE CHURCH

by Lynley Mandrell

First, read Ephesians 2:14-19.

As a pastor's wife, I have seen so many beautiful things happen in the local church, but today's topic on peace reminds me of the needless feuds that often develop too. Christians sometimes waste a lot of energy fighting one another. This is not a new problem. Even a quick glance at the New Testament reveals how many times Paul addressed the bickering inside church families. If we aren't careful, the watching world will roll their eyes as we run one another down.

Perhaps you're reading this and you are not a churchgoer for this very reason. You are not alone. In 2013, our family packed up and moved cross-country to plant a church. When we planted our church in Denver, we talked to a lot of nonreligious people who were turned off to the church because of the infighting. It is sort of ironic, isn't it? We claim to know the Prince of peace, and yet many of our churches are filled with strife.

Soon after we moved into our house, we became friends with many of our neighbors. It didn't take long for them to open up about their feelings toward Christians. For example, one gentleman commented that a lady at work who was quite vocal about her Christian faith was also the sender of scathing emails, and, in general, the thorn in everyone's flesh. "My nonreligious teammates care more about my life than the one who claims to know Jesus," he said. Another woman we met had a sad story of hurt from her family's past. Both of her churchgoing grandfathers had extramarital affairs with women inside the church, which left a wake of devastation for their families.

I know, I know. Let me stop here and say that stereotyping is so unfair. However, the point still rings true: our actions do speak louder than our words. When unbelievers watch us picking on one another, they oftentimes don't have the opportunity to see the resolution and to witness the grace extended. Keeping the peace in the church is mission critical.

Today's passage from Ephesians is a challenge to us all. In this part of the letter, Paul was unpacking the reality that Jesus has placed Jews and Gentiles into one gospel-centered family. Paul was calling the Ephesian believers (and us!) to unite and move forward together for the sake of the gospel, regardless of the past.

What is all this "Jew and Gentile" talk? If you are new to the Bible, then these categories likely mean nothing to you. Why did the Jews have a problem with the Gentiles anyway? And why did these two groups refuse to mix?

The answer: engrained tradition. For centuries the Jews practiced certain customs, cherished particular practices, and held to certain life rhythms. All those "unusual" people who didn't follow suit were considered foreigners (not part of the group). To the Jews, the Gentiles didn't show enough respect for their history.

Traditions become part of the fabric of who we are and are painfully difficult to shed.

Does this spark any thoughts of life in your local church? Write them below.

Healthy churches draw people from all traditions, ages, ethnic groups, and worship preferences. With this level of diversity in the room, disagreement is bound to happen. If you find yourself feuding with fellow church members, here are three questions to consider.

1. Have you gotten involved before giving suggestions?

At our church in Denver, I served as the director of kids ministry. Suffice it to say, I fielded a few complaints over the years. The objections most difficult to swallow were from those who chose not to serve. Sure, there are exceptions. Key volunteers also offered ideas for ministry improvement, but it is far easier to receive feedback from those who have sought to understand the processes in place. Seek to understand before seeking to be understood.

READ MATTHEW 20:28.

How does this passage inform your role within your local church?

2. Is this about the Bible or is it about a personal preference?

One question we often forget to ask is this: what does the Bible say on this subject? Consider the volume of the music, the look of the building, the style of the kids programming—in each of these cases, and so many more, there is no chapter and verse to guide us. So what should we do? We pray, asking God for wisdom (Jas. 1:5), and then we think generously and remember that sometimes we don't get what we want. Isn't that the case with all healthy families?

READ EPHESIANS 5:19-21.

How does this passage encourage us to interact with our fellow Christ followers?

3. Are you peacemaking or peace-faking?

In his classic book *The Peacemaker*, Ken Sande distinguishes between peacemaking and peace-faking.[21] Peacemakers approach others in a spirit of reconciliation, hoping to find a solution to a problem and to reach a place of peace. Peace-fakers, on the other hand, come in a spirit of selfishness, assuming that the answer to the problem will meet their expectations, even if it is not the best answer for all. Sadly, a peace-faker will often give the impression that all is well, but behind closed doors this person is stirring up discord.

When it comes to your church family, are you among the peacemakers?

To end today's study, write out Matthew 5:9 as a prayer for your church.

GOSPEL TO THE GENTILES

by Carol Pipes

𝔉irst, read 𝔄cts 10:34-43.

I love decorating my Christmas tree. Unwrapping each ornament from its tissue-paper cocoon evokes a walk down memory lane. Every glass ball and plastic figurine has a story. Even the funky felt horse head with its glitter mane crafted in kindergarten is a treasure. But my favorite ornaments are the ones my husband, Keith, and I have collected from locations around the globe where we've served alongside local churches.

Several years ago, we began to lead short-term mission trips for high school and college students. We've built houses in New Orleans, served refugees in Greece, and led cooking classes in Ecuador, all for the chance to share the gospel. We have an ornament from every city where we've served—an intentional reminder to pray for the people who have yet to hear the gospel and for the local believers who live on mission every day. Those decorations represent precious people and serve as a visual reminder that Jesus came to bring hope and peace to people from every nation.

Just as each ornament on my tree is unique, each trip has been distinct in the work we've done and the people we've served. But the constant thread connecting each trip has been the unity found among God's people.

We've experienced instant connections with members of the body of Christ around the world. Language barriers cannot thwart the Spirit in me recognizing the Spirit in another believer. Only through Jesus Christ can we find such community and harmony among strangers.

> Can you think of a time when you've recognized the Spirit of God in someone you just met?

Two days ago, we read God's promise to Abram that all the peoples on earth would be blessed through him.

REREAD GENESIS 12:3.

In the Book of Acts, we begin to see that promise fulfilled. The first chapters of Acts describe the beginnings of the church in Jerusalem. Then in Acts 8, we read that the believers in Jerusalem were scattered throughout Judea and Samaria because of intense persecution. And it's in Acts where we first see the gospel carried across ethnic and national boundaries—spreading to the Gentiles.

In Acts 10, we find the apostle Peter lodging at Simon the tanner's house in Joppa. He was up on the roof praying when he fell into a trance. He saw an object resembling a large sheet being lowered from heaven. In the sheet were animals, reptiles, and birds all deemed unclean, and therefore inedible, by Jewish law. A voice told Peter to kill and eat the animals. Peter refused, as this would have been a violation of Jewish law.

Write Acts 10:15 below.

This back and forth happened three times before the object was taken up into heaven. Imagine the conflict Peter must have felt.

If we keep reading, we discover that Peter was still thinking about the vision when three men from Caesarea showed up looking for him. They'd been sent by Cornelius, a Gentile, to find Peter and bring him back to Caesarea. Prompted by the Holy Spirit, Peter agreed to go with them. Although it was forbidden for a Jewish man to associate with a Gentile, Peter entered Cornelius' home. Peter realized the vision was God's way of showing him that he should not consider any person impure or unclean.

Write down Peter's words found in Acts 10:34.

Are there any people you believe don't deserve God's gift of salvation?

Do you have any prejudices, or even preferences, that would keep you from developing relationships and sharing the gospel with particular people groups?

What would need to change in your heart for you to open your heart and mind to those groups?

Acts records that word began to spread among the Jewish believers that Gentiles had responded to the gospel. The Jewish believers in Jerusalem heard about Peter's visit with Cornelius and were critical that Peter had entered the house of uncircumcised men and eaten with them. The Jews saw this as a compromise of God's laws. Peter explained to them everything that had happened: his vision in Joppa, his visit with Cornelius, and how God had given the Gentiles the gift of the Holy Spirit. When the Jewish Christians heard Peter's defense, they praised God, saying, "So then, God has given repentance resulting in life even to the Gentiles" (Acts 11:18).

What false qualifications are you holding others to? Are you adding anything (human traditions, religious acts, etc.) to the gospel?

The gospel continued to spread beyond Judea to places as far away as Antioch. The church in Antioch became a missionary sending center—sending Paul on his missionary journeys further spreading the gospel to Europe.

READ ACTS 13:47-49.

Hallelujah! We can rejoice that God sent His Son, Jesus, to bring salvation to all peoples—Jews and Gentiles, you and me. The gospel is God's power to save all who believe. But how will people believe if they never hear? And how will they hear if someone doesn't go and tell them (Rom. 10:14)? God sends believers, His church, into the world with a distinct message of love, redemption, and abundant life found only in Jesus Christ. We are commanded by God and empowered by the Holy Spirit to join God in His mission to spread the gospel to all people!

> If you are a follower of Jesus, how might you be a light for others and point to salvation through Jesus Christ? Pray the Lord will open a door for you to share the good news of Christ's birth, death, and resurrection with various people groups living in your community. Ask God to open your eyes to opportunities around you. God means for us to live sent. Let the love of God that dwells within compel you to step out on mission with Him.

GOSPEL SPREAD

by Deborah Spooner

First, read Matthew 28:18-20.

"What is your mission?"

I remember being asked this question as a young adult. It felt vast and daunting and so very important. Some of us have wrestled with this while others may not have fully stopped to consider personal mission. Yet as followers of Christ, we know our mission involves the Lord. Regardless of the specific ways the Lord has for each of us to serve Him, we all share a common, big picture mission which comes from the Great Commission.

Jesus, the Desire of nations, was fully focused on doing what His Father had sent Him to do (John 17:4). Emmanuel, God with us, came to be the sacrifice the world desperately needed.

As we seek to follow Jesus in the mission of spreading the gospel, we must first be fueled by the reality that God has come near to us. As we sing the words of "O come, O come, Emmanuel," we're celebrating that Jesus has come to reconcile us to God and to empower us to continue to spread the message of gospel reconciliation to others (2 Cor. 5:11-21). We can fulfill the Great Commission because we've been filled with His Spirit to declare the power of the gospel.

REVIEW MATTHEW 28:19.

What two commands did Jesus give?

Jesus commissioned His original disciples to be heralds of the good news by going and making disciples. He calls us to do likewise.

REVIEW MATTHEW 28:20a.

What are disciples supposed to teach the new disciples they are making?

How has obedience to the Lord impacted you personally as a disciple?

We are stronger in community. If we are going to spread gospel hope, we must function as the body of Christ. No human body is made up of just one part, and the body of Christ is no exception (1 Cor. 12:14).

READ JOHN 13:35 AND GALATIANS 6:2.

How are disciples of Christ identified according to these passages?

We can experience growth in community that we can't on our own. We care for each other in community. And our community is one of the biggest witnesses to the gospel.

REVIEW MATTHEW 28:20b.

After Jesus gave the Great Commission to His disciples, what hope-filled thought did He leave with them?

Jesus is with us. *Always.* Our motivation for making disciples starts with remembering the One who came to us, and we rest in the reality that His Spirit remains with us.

How does remembering that the Lord is always with you empower you to make disciples?

The heart of the Great Commission and the heart of our Christian walk is Christ. We start with Him as we are compelled by His love coming to us (2 Cor. 5:14-15). We desire to follow the Desire of nations, and we do this through helping form worshipful, obedient Christ followers. Then, we join our personal devotion to Christ with other disciples devoted to Him, caring for one another, bearing with each other, persevering through difficulties, and celebrating joys. Together, we remember that He is with us even as we wait to be with Him in the coming marriage supper of the Lamb.

Lord, remind us that we cannot go and make disciples if we don't first come to You and thank You for what You came to do on the cross. Teach us what it means to follow You as a disciple. Show us how to live out our mission of spreading the gospel and making other disciples. Guide us to remember Your nearness as the collective body of Christ.

EVERY TRIBE AND TONGUE AND NATION

by Chelsea Collins

First, read Revelation 7:9-10.

Throughout this study we have looked at certain attributes of Jesus as we prepare to celebrate His birth at Christmas. In the first week, we learned that God has been with us from the beginning and will be with us for all eternity. During the second week we learned about Jesus our Dayspring—our light and hope—to help us understand the darkness of this world and inside ourselves. In the third week studying together we read about how Jesus is the wisdom of God and how we have to rely on Him for wisdom, not our own ideas. This last week we are reflecting on Jesus as the Desire of nations. Jesus came to save once and for all and to give life to people from every nation.

Revelation 7:9-10 contains a portion of John's vision while he was exiled on the island of Patmos. God gave John instructions to give to seven churches in Asia Minor, but more than that, God gave John an extended glimpse into what eternity in heaven might look like.

In these verses, whom did John say he saw?

How many people were there?

What were they doing?

What were they saying?

Verse 9 tells us the people around the throne were "from every nation, tribe, people, and language." Remember from Day 3 this week that God commissioned Peter and His other disciples to share the gospel with everyone, Jews and Gentiles.

> Beside each passage below, write down the words related to sharing the gospel with other nations.
>
> • Matthew 28:19-20
>
> • Mark 16:15
>
> • John 3:16
>
> What do all these verses have in common?

Consider the fourth verse of the hymn, "O Come, O Come, Emmanuel":

O Come, Desire of nations,

bind all peoples in one heart and mind;

Bid envy, strife, and quarrels cease;

Fill the whole world with heaven's peace.[22]

It is clear that we are to share the gospel with all people regardless of their nationality, language, or heritage. We know that the sins of discrimination and racism are rampant in our culture, but as Christians, Jesus instructs us to love our neighbors as ourselves (Matt. 19:19b). Just as we serve one God, if we are in Christ, we are one body no matter the language we speak or the color of our skin. Our unity points to the peace found only in Christ. Not only are we called to unity here on earth, John's revelation reveals that when we are reunited with Jesus in the new heaven and new earth, we will worship God in perfect unity forever. Amen! How beautiful it will be when we are all together in eternity!

Read Haggai 2:7 (CSB) and fill in the blank.

"I will shake all the nations so that the _____ of all the nations will come, and I will fill this house with glory."

This word from the Lord to the prophet Haggai was, according to some scholars, a prophecy about Jesus and His future entry into the temple. When God referred to the "treasures" of all the nations, (or your translation might say "desire"), He wasn't referring to a general peace but to the Prince of peace—Jesus!

Jesus wants all people to find peace in Him, and we, as His followers, are His instruments in carrying out the gospel of peace.

Is the desire of your heart to see people from all nations join you in eternity?

Other than mission trips, what are some ways you can be a part in spreading the gospel around the world?

REVIEW REVELATION 7:10.

The great multitude was standing before the throne and the Lamb worshiping. They cried out in unison. Instead of multiple voices, John heard a singular voice praising God.

In your own words, summarize what they said in worship.

There is nothing we can do to earn our salvation. We can only receive it because God extended it to us through Jesus' death on the cross. When Jesus returns to receive His bride, the church, it will not be because of our good deeds but because God has deemed it the exact time He wants to rescue His children. It is at that time Jesus will allow those who have accepted His salvation to step into eternity and perfect peace with him.

Jesus has extended hope to you as part of the "nations." How have you seen that kindness extended in your life (in salvation but also in other gracious ways)?

How has this study prepared your heart to celebrate Christmas this year?

As you close your time with this study in prayer today, thank God for sending His Son to reconcile us back to Him. Ask God to show you ways you can help spread the gospel to every tribe and tongue and nation. Pray for those souls around the world who are looking for peace in their lives, that they would find Jesus and declare Him their hope in a dark world.

NOTES

Cookie Exchange

by Larissa Arnault Roach

Jesus came to bring hope to every person on earth—every tribe, every tongue, every nation. The love of Christ should overflow from us to those around us. We are people of celebration, so celebrate with cookies from around the world! This is a great opportunity to invite believers, nonbelievers, and I-don't-know-what-I-believers so you can extend the kindness of your salvation to others this Christmas.

At a cookie exchange, each guest brings one kind of cookie but leaves with dozens of different cookies to enjoy. What's not to love? There are just two difficult things about hosting a cookie swap: 1) This is a party with instructions, and you will need a firm yes or no from those you invite; and 2) There is some math involved.

If you plan to have ten guests, including yourself, and each guest is to sample cookies (Let's say you eat ten cookies at the party—Merry Christmas to you.) as well as take 6 of each kind of cookie home, everyone will need to bake 70 cookies. Each person will sample 10 cookies (1 from each person's batch) at the party and each person will take home 60 cookies. You'll ask each guest to bake 70 cookies because (10x6)+10=70. Adjust this equation based on the number of guests you plan to invite.

$$\left(\begin{array}{c} \text{\# of people} \\ \text{at the party} \end{array} \times \begin{array}{c} \text{\# of cookies} \\ \text{you want to} \\ \text{take home} \end{array} \right) + \begin{array}{c} \text{\# of samples} \\ \text{you'll want to} \\ \text{eat at the party} \end{array} = \begin{array}{c} \text{how many cookies} \\ \text{each person will need} \\ \text{to bring to the party} \end{array}$$

DIRECTIONS

1. Think of a variety of people to invite. Six to twelve is ideal.
2. Assign each guest a country to use as the inspiration for the cookie they will bring. This should also ensure there are no duplicate cookies.
3. Do the math, and tell your guests exactly how many cookies to bring to the party. Ask them to package their cookies in individual bags or containers of six each.
4. Leaving with the cookies is great, but passing along the recipes is even better! Depending on your group, you can ask guests to print copies of their recipes for people to take home.

As you bake your cookies, pray for people of the world to know Christ. On the day of the party, set up a table to display everyone's cookies. Consider giving out fun prizes (like tea towels, spatulas, and oven mitts) for the prettiest cookies, the largest, the most unique, and the biggest flavor.

TASTES OF THE
Nations

by Michelle Prater Freeman

We want a lot at Christmastime ... the right deal on a gift, time with family, and a moment of peace among the chaos of red and green. But Scripture tells us what humans worldwide long for the most: Jesus, "the desire of all nations" (Hag. 2:7, KJV).

December focuses a lot on Jesus' birth in the tiny town of Bethlehem, but it's helpful to remember that He came for people near and far, both Jew and Gentile. In the parable of the good Samaritan, Jesus preached the message of unity, and Psalm 22:28 tells us that He rules over all the nations.

Christmas is the perfect time to remind your teen, and yourself, that Jesus didn't just come for the people who look like us or live near us. He came for all nations. People worldwide mark His coming with us each Christmas, and one day they will bow with us as well. This shared kinship is worth celebrating and exploring.

A few years ago, I joined friends at an Ethiopian restaurant, where I discovered tastes and textures I didn't know even existed! It was a fun introduction to a people and culture that were new to me. To encourage your teen to celebrate God's love for the world this December, you might try the same. Forgo the typical spaghetti night and choose a restaurant or recipe that explores an entirely different palate and a cuisine from a faraway land.

Try a kabob koobideh at a Persian restaurant. Discover Filipino fare such as pancit. Or gather in the kitchen to make alfajores, Argentinian Christmas cookies. Then, as you munch, talk about the rich variety of cultures and faces among God's people. As a family, thank Jesus that He was willing to be the Desire of all nations, and that one day we might all join Him. Together.

CHRISTMAS CARD
Missionaries

by Shelly D. Harris

The Jewish people had waited and longed for their Messiah to come. Jesus came to rescue God's people, Israel, but He also came to rescue the rest of the world. Hallelujah!

Jesus is the Desire of nations. We long for the peace and hope found only in Jesus. We can celebrate that we know and understand that Jesus came to rescue us from our sin. Jesus made a way for everyone to have a relationship with God when He sacrificed His life by dying on the cross to pay for our sin. One day Jesus will come again and people from every tribe, language, and nation will realize that He is the King of kings. If we have repented of our sin and trusted Jesus as our Lord and Savior, we will spend eternity worshiping Jesus. Invite family members to ask any questions they have about the gospel.

As followers of Jesus, we are called to share the gospel with others. Make a list of people your family wants to share the gospel with. Talk about ways your family can reach out to each person on your list throughout the next few months. Select at least one person to begin building a friendship (or better friendship) with.

DIRECTIONS

Gather various colors of cardstock, Christmas-themed stickers, markers, and scissors. Invite everyone to create a Christmas card for one of your neighbors, friends, or family members. Encourage everyone to print John 3:16, Romans 5:8, or other gospel truths inside their cards. As a family, visit each person you made a card for, and sing a Christmas carol for them while delivering your card. (Consider practicing and singing "O Come, O Come, Emmanuel.")

Conclude by praying together: *Thank You, God, for sending Jesus to rescue our world from sin. We praise You because You are the source of hope and peace. Please help us continue to tell others about You and your gift of salvation. Amen.*

wrap-up

UNTIL THE SON OF GOD APPEARS

by Erin Franklin

We've covered a lot in our time together, learning how God has been—and will always be—with us, and how Christ is our Dayspring, our Wisdom, and the Desire of nations. We know the story, including what comes next.

At the beginning of the study, we saw that the lyrics of "O Come, O Come Emmanuel" serve a dual purpose, aptly applying both to Israel's hope for Christ's first coming and also our hope as we await His second coming. As we remember Christ's birth this Advent season, we long for His return. We celebrate the new life in Christ we have, yet we still hope for a place with no more grief, no more pain, no more death. Through the promise of salvation, this hope will be fulfilled at His return (Rev. 21:4).

Perhaps early on in your walk with Jesus, you, like me, had thoughts similar to these when thinking about Christ's return: *But wait—first, I want to go on my vacation next week. I want to go to college. I want to get married and have kids and grandkids. I want to do all the things you (older Christians) have been able to do before Jesus comes back.* As faith matures, though, our understanding of heaven develops to a deeper comprehension that goes beyond worldly desires. But now, why do we primarily want Jesus to return? Is it the yearning to be reunited with family members? The hungering for a world of peace? While it's true and good that we may look forward to all these things, we must remember not to place them above the simple yet primary longing to be with Christ forever, worshiping Him.

We can't celebrate His first coming this Advent season without also being ready to celebrate His second coming above all else. We rejoice because God is with us, indwelling us with His Holy Spirit and fully knowing us as His children. Yet we "eagerly wait" (Phil. 3:20) for the day when the Light of the world will come to eradicate darkness and fully reveal the glory of God to us "face to face" (1 Cor. 13:12).

So because we know the rest of the story, we can share the rest of the story. Not only is Advent a time of celebrating and rejoicing in the present with our brothers and sisters in Christ, but it's also a time to share the gospel hope with those who don't yet know His redeeming love personally. The purpose of His birth, death, and resurrection is so that all who believe in Him can be saved before His return to earth as King, when perfect justice and judgment will be enacted (John 3:16; Matt. 25:31-46).

The reality of the goodness found in walking with Emmanuel's guiding light and wisdom leads to a desire to share this good news with all people—so that each can say with profound hope and faith, "O come, O come, Emmanuel!"

How has the reality that Jesus is Emmanuel, God with us, shaped your Advent season this year?

What specific passages of Scripture have taken on new life for you during these weeks of study?

In what areas of your life are you still needing hope? How can we specifically pray for you?

How can Christians use the Christmas season to boldly declare the hope of the gospel?

Write down the names of any nonbelievers the Lord brings to mind. Pray through those names as a group, asking God to reveal Himself to the individuals mentioned. Pray that they would give their hearts to Him and experience His presence in their lives.

CONTRIBUTORS

JOY ALLMOND

Joy Allmond serves on LifeWay's corporate communications team and is the managing editor of *Facts & Trends*, LifeWay's online magazine geared toward church leaders.

W. DIANE BRADEN

W. Diane Braden attended Tennessee State University majoring in Journalism. She has been employed with LifeWay for the last twenty years. She is married to the love of her life, Ronald, and together they founded Holy Reconciliation Ministries birthed out of their testimony of marriage reconciliation.

CHELSEA COLLINS

Chelsea Collins is the editor for *LifeWay Mujeres* and works with Hispanic women all over the world to create content for women. She and her husband, Chris, live with their two fur babies, Marlee and Nala. Chelsea earned a Bachelors degree from Union University in Spanish and loves that she is able use it every day. Chelsea enjoys afternoon naps, reading, and traveling whenever she can.

SARAH DOSS

Sarah Doss is the Team Leader for LifeWay's Adult Ministry Short Term Bible study team. With an educational background in communications from the University of Georgia, this Georgia peach now calls Nashville home. In her spare time, Sarah enjoys watching quirky sitcoms, a strong cup of coffee, and travel (international or otherwise).

RACHEL FORREST

Rachel Forrest is a writer who pursues to tell the truth as beautifully as she can. She lives in Oklahoma with her husband and two children. She has an M.A. in theological studies and works for LifeWay as an eBook Developer. You can find her online at www.rachelleaforrest.com.

ERIN FRANKLIN

Erin Franklin is a production editor at LifeWay and is a graduate of Lipscomb University. The Tennessee native is passionate about communication and enjoys spending time on her family's century farm, meeting new people, and playing a good ping-pong match. You can connect with her on Instagram @erin_franklin and on Twitter @erinefranklin.

CONTRIBUTORS

MICHELLE PRATER FREEMAN

Michelle Prater Freeman is the publisher of kid and teen books for B&H. She and her family make their home in Mt. Juliet, Tennessee.

VALERIE HANCOCK

Valerie Hancock is a writer and editor living in Nashville. She is the content strategist for LifeWay.com.

SHELLY D. HARRIS

Shelly D. Harris serves as a content editor for LifeWay Kids. She is a graduate of Murray State University and the Southern Baptist Theological Seminary. As a former kids minister, Shelly is passionate about equipping the church and families to share the gospel and disciple kids. She currently serves as a girl's small group leader at The Bridge in Spring Hill, Tennessee.

MORGAN HAWK

Morgan Hawk holds a master's degree in publishing. She serves as an editor for LifeWay Students. Morgan brings laughter, stability, and endless book recommendations to her coworkers. She is currently leading a group of ninth grade girls at her church in Brentwood. Morgan's favorite things include big dogs, cupcakes, and afternoon naps.

ELIZABETH HYNDMAN

Elizabeth Hyndman reads, writes, and tweets. Officially, she's a social media strategist at LifeWay where she uses both her English undergraduate and her seminary graduate degrees every day. Elizabeth grew up in Nashville, sips chai lattes every chance she can get, and believes everyone should have a "funny picture" pose at the ready. Follow her on Twitter or Instagram at @edhyndman.

CATHERINE INMAN

Catherine Inman is the event project coordinator for women's leadership training events at LifeWay. Prior to her current role, she served as girls ministry director and a missionary in Europe, Africa, and Asia. Catherine is passionate about biblical literacy and equipping women to reach their full potential in Christ.

CONTRIBUTORS

LARISSA ARNAULT ROACH

Larissa Arnault Roach is the marketing manager for LifeWay Women. She loves butter, books, and bright lipstick. Always up for a special meal—Christmas or otherwise—she considers Ecclesiastes 2:24-25 her life verses. Larissa lives in downtown Nashville with her husband Nate, daughter Eliza, son Ozark, and dog Margot.

DEBORAH SPOONER

Deborah Spooner is a Minnesota-born analytical creative serving as a marketing strategist for LifeWay's Groups team. As a pastor's daughter with a background in digital communications and media and biblical and theological studies, you can find her at her local church, in deep conversations, or with a book or pen in hand as she seeks to know Christ more and make Him known.

AMANDA MAE STEELE

Amanda Mae Steele is a writer, photographer, and performing artist based in Franklin, Tennessee. She lives with her husband, Nick, and their eleven-year-old "puppy," Dino. She is passionate about God's Word, other cultures, and sharing the gospel mostly through silly (but relatable) personal anecdotes. She serves as the B&H Kids marketing specialist.

FAITH C. WHATLEY

Faith C. Whatley serves LifeWay as the director of author and strategic partnerships. She came to LifeWay in 1991 and has led many significant ministries. She has spent many years devoted to ministry to women at LifeWay. Faith has been married to Jimmy for thirty-three years. Together, they have two grown children and two precious grandsons who hold their hearts.

ELLEN WILDMAN

Ellen Wildman is a Bible marketing specialist at LifeWay. She holds a B.A. in Bible and ministry to women from Moody Bible Institute and is currently pursuing a master's at Denver Seminary. Ellen lives in Nashville, and in her free time, she enjoys studying baking bread, reading the latest book club pick, and grabbing chai lattes with friends.

JESSICA YENTZER

Jessica Yentzer is a marketing strategist on LifeWay's Adult Ministry team. Well-written memoirs, dark chocolate, a good running trail, and the perfect fall day are just a few of the things that put a smile on her face. When she's not planning marketing strategy, she loves hiking and exploring the outdoors with her husband, Grant.

ERIN IVEY

Erin Ivey serves as the marketing manager for the LifeWay Groups team. She's a native Nashvillian living in Brentwood, Tennessee, with her husband, Carter, and their adorable and spunky miniature schnauzer, Rosie. When she's not working, she spends her day drinking coffee, reading a good book, hiking at Radnor lake, and cheering on her Mississippi State Bulldogs with family and friends.

KELLY D. KING

Kelly D. King is the manager of the magazine and devotional team and women's ministry training for LifeWay. She enjoys being the cohost of LifeWay's *Marked* podcast and is the author of *Ministry to Women: The Essential Guide to Leading Women in the Local Church.* She holds a master's degree from Gateway Seminary. While Nashville is where she lives, she still claims Oklahoma as her home.

KAREN JONES

Karen Jones serves at LifeWay as the preschool content editor for *The Gospel Project* curriculum. She came to LifeWay in 2014 with over fifteen years of experience in preschool and children's ministry. Karen earned an M.A. in Christian education from New Orleans Baptist Theological Seminary. She enjoys teaching preschoolers and leading a women's discipleship group at Immanuel Church.

LYNLEY MANDRELL

Lynley Mandrell is the wife of Ben Mandrell, the president and CEO of LifeWay. Before coming to LifeWay, Ben and Lynley spent five years in Denver, Colorado, planting a church designed to reach the unchurched. She is a mother of four and a fan of Reese's Peanut Butter Cups, Dr. Pepper, and silence.

RAVIN MCKELVY

Ravin McKelvy is a copywriter at LifeWay and graduated with a degree in communications from Moody Bible Institute. She is passionate about the intersection of art and theology and sharing the daily realities of Christian living on Instagram. She grew up in a family of twelve and currently lives with some of her family in Franklin, Tennessee.

CAROL PIPES

Carol Pipes is director of corporate communications at LifeWay and senior editor of *Facts & Trends.* She has worked in Christian publishing for nearly twenty years, during which time she has written numerous magazine articles and previously served as editor of *On Mission* magazine. A Tennessee native, Carol lives in Nashville with her husband, Keith, who leads the music ministry team at Friendship Community Church.

LIGHT A CANDLE

In the Christian tradition, many light a candle each week of Advent. You may have seen this take place in churches around the world. We light the candles during Advent to represent the Light who has come into the world, Jesus (Isa. 9:6). As we mark each week leading up to Advent, we also consider the themes that surround the season, all of which we root in Jesus' coming to earth—hope, peace, joy, and love. If you would like to participate in this tradition in your home, we've provided a quick guide for you below.

Week 1: Hope

As you light the candle this week, prayerfully consider the hope God brings to the world and read the following passage.

> The people walking in darkness have seen a great light; a light has dawned on those living in the land of darkness.
>
> Isaiah 9:2

Week 2: Peace

As you light the candle this week, prayerfully consider God's peace coming into our hearts and minds and the peace Jesus brings between us and God. Then read the following passage.

> For a child will be born for us, a son will be given to us, and the government will be on his shoulders. He will be named Wonderful Counselor, Mighty God, Eternal Father, Prince of Peace.
>
> Isaiah 9:6

Week 3: Joy

As you light the candle this week, meditate on the incomparable joy that we can know in God alone and read the following passage.

> After seeing them, they reported the message they were told about this child, and all who heard it were amazed at what the shepherds said to them.
>
> Luke 2:17-18

Week 4: Love

As you light the candle this week, meditate on God's unconditional love for us all year long by reading the following passage.

> For God loved the world in this way: He gave his one and only Son, so that everyone who believes in him will not perish but have eternal life. For God did not send his Son into the world to condemn the world, but to save the world through him.
>
> John 3:16-17

ENDNOTES

WEEK 1

1. John Mason Neale, trans., "O Come, O Come, Emmanuel," Baptist Hymnal (Convention Press, 1991), 76.

2. *Ibid.*

3. "*Qadash*," Strong's H6942, Blue Letter Bible. Available online at BlueLetterBible.com.

4. Robert Stein, *New American Commentary: Luke*, vol. 24 (Nashville, TN: B&H Publishing Group, 2012).

5. "*Skēnoō*," Strong's G4637, Blue Letter Bible. Available online at BlueLetterBible.com.

6. *Menō*," Strong's G3306, Blue Letter Bible. Available online at BlueLetterBible.com.

WEEK 2

7. John Mason Neale, trans., "O Come, O Come, Emmanuel," Baptist Hymnal (Convention Press, 1991), 76.

8. *Merriam Webster*, s.v. "Futile," June 8, 2020, https://www.merriam-webster.com/dictionary/futile.

9. Max Anders, Kenneth Boa and William Kruidenier, *Holman New Testament Commentary: Romans,* vol. 6 (Nashville, TN: B&H Publishing Group, 2012).

10. Marc Lawrence, Katie Ford, and Caryn Lucas. *Miss Congeniality*. Directed by Donald Petrie. Los Angeles: Warner Bros. Pictures, 2000.

11. Spencer Parlier and Christina Zdanowicz. "This Alaskan town won't see the sun for 65 days." CNN.com. https://www.cnn.com/2018/11/20/us/alaskan-town-no-sun-trnd/index.html, accessed June 8, 2020.

12. "*Owr,*" Strong's H216, Blue Letter Bible. Available online at BlueLetterBible.com.

13. John Mason Neale, trans., "O Come, O Come, Emmanuel," Baptist Hymnal (Convention Press, 1991), 76

14. "*Phos*," Strong's G5457, Blue Letter Bible. Available online at BlueLetterBible.com.

WEEK 3

15. John Mason Neale, trans., "O Come, O Come, Emmanuel," Baptist Hymnal (Convention Press, 1991), 76.

16. R. C. Sproul, *Knowing Scripture* (Downers Grove, IL: InterVarsity Press, 1977).

17. Matthew Henry, *Matthew Henry Commentary on the Whole Bible*, Colossians 2. Available online at BibleStudyTools.com.

18. "*Exagorazo,*" Strong's G1805. Blue Letter Bible. Available online at BlueLetterBible.com.

19. Adapted from DearMuska.com. System originated from SimplyCharlotteMason.com.

WEEK 4

20. John Mason Neale, trans., "O Come, O Come, Emmanuel," Baptist Hymnal (Convention Press, 1991), 76.

21. Ken Sande, *The Peacemaker: A Biblical Guide to Resolving Personal Conflict* (Grand Rapids, MI: Baker Books, 2004), 28.

22. John Mason Neale, trans., "O Come, O Come, Emmanuel," Baptist Hymnal (Convention Press, 1991), 76.

BECOMING A CHRISTIAN

Romans 10:17 says, "So faith comes from what is heard, and what is heard comes through the message about Christ."

Maybe you've stumbled across new information in this study. Or maybe you've attended church all your life, but something you read here struck you differently than it ever has before. If you have never accepted Christ but would like to, read on to discover how you can become a Christian.

Your heart tends to run from God and rebel against Him. The Bible calls this *sin*. Romans 3:23 says, "For all have sinned and fall short of the glory of God."

Yet God loves you and wants to save you from sin, to offer you a new life of hope. John 10:10b says, "I have come so that they may have life and have it in abundance."

To give you this gift of salvation, God made a way through His Son, Jesus Christ. Romans 5:8 says, "But God proves his own love for us in that while we were still sinners, Christ died for us."

You receive this gift by faith alone. Ephesians 2:8-9 says, "For you are saved by grace through faith, and this not from yourselves; it is God's gift—not from works, so that no one can boast."

Faith is a decision of your heart demonstrated by the actions of your life. Romans 10:9 says, "If you confess with your mouth, 'Jesus is Lord,' and believe in your heart that God raised him from the dead, you will be saved."

If you trust that Jesus died for your sins and want to receive new life through Him, pray a prayer similar to the following to express your repentance and faith in Him:

"DEAR GOD, I KNOW I AM A SINNER. I BELIEVE JESUS DIED TO FORGIVE ME OF MY SINS. I ACCEPT YOUR OFFER OF ETERNAL LIFE. THANK YOU FOR FORGIVING ME OF ALL MY SINS. THANK YOU FOR MY NEW LIFE. FROM THIS DAY FORWARD, I WILL CHOOSE TO FOLLOW YOU."

If you have trusted Jesus for salvation, please share your decision with your group leader or another Christian friend. If you are not already attending church, find one in which you can worship and grow in your faith. Following Christ's example, ask to be baptized as a public expression of your faith.

LET'S BE FRIENDS!

BLOG

We're here to help you grow in your faith, develop as a leader, and find encouragement as you go.

LifeWayWomen.com

SOCIAL

Find inspiration in the in-between moments of life.

@LifeWayWomen

NEWSLETTER

Be the first to hear about new studies, events, giveaways, and more by signing up.

LifeWay.com/ WomensNews

LifeWay | Women